WATERSIDE WALKS
In Sussex

Ben Perkins

COUNTRYSIDE BOOKS
NEWBURY, BERKSHIRE

First published 1999

Reprinted 2000

COUNTRYSIDE BOOKS
3 Catherine Road
Newbury, Berkshire

To view our complete range of books,
please visit us at
www.countrysidebooks.co.uk

ISBN 1 85306 570 6

Designed by Graham Whiteman
Cover illustration by Colin Doggett
Maps and photographs by the author

Produced through MRM Associates Ltd., Reading
Typeset by Techniset Typesetters, Newton-le-Willows
Printed by Woolnough Bookbinding Ltd., Irthlingborough

Contents

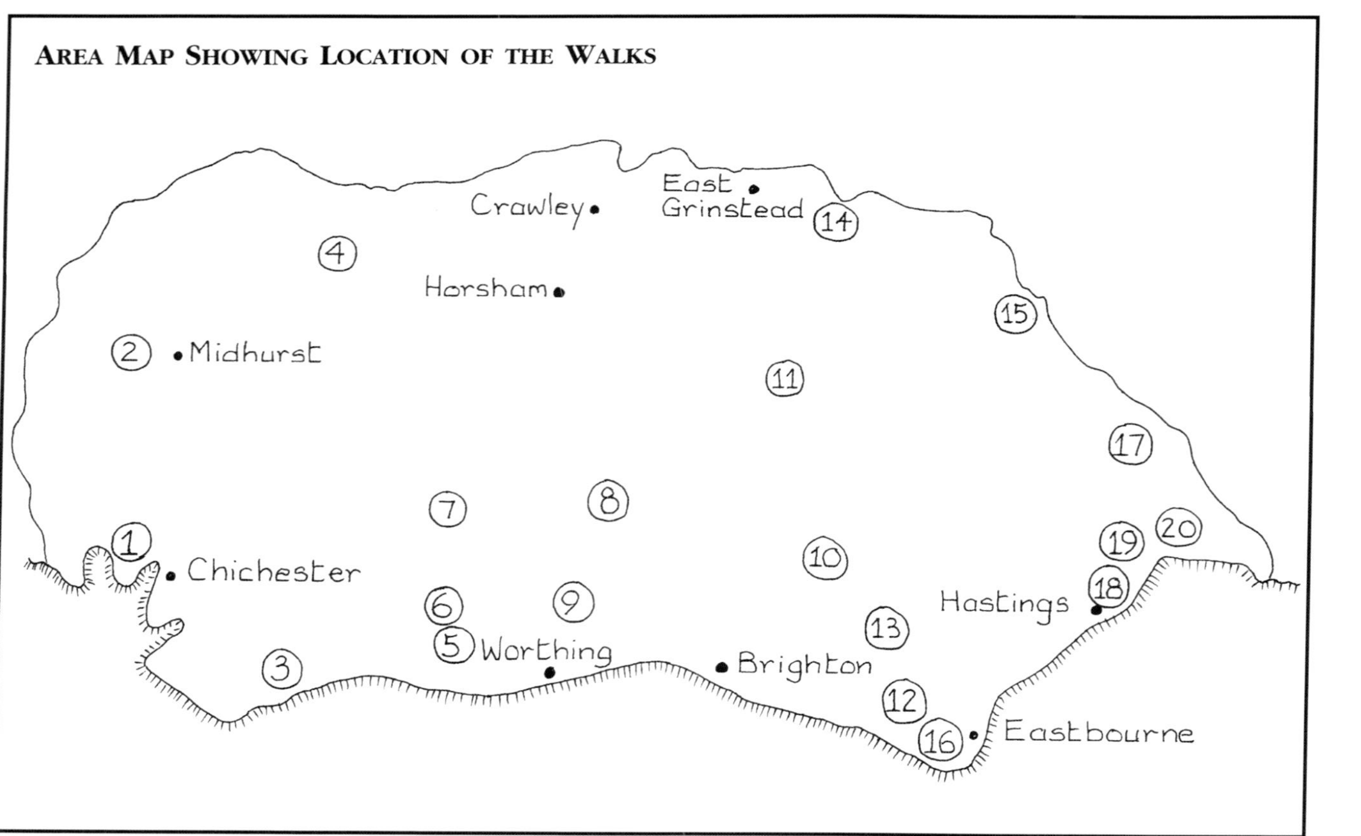
Area Map Showing Location of the Walks
East
Grinstead
Crawley
Horsham
Midhurst
Chichester
Worthing
Brighton
Hastings
Eastbourne
1
2
3
4
5
6
7
8
9
10
11
12
13
14
15
16
17
18
19
20

Walk

Publisher's Note

We hope that you obtain considerable enjoyment from this book; great care has been taken in its preparation. Although at the time of publication all routes followed public rights of way or permitted paths, diversion orders can be made and permissions withdrawn.

We cannot of course be held responsible for such diversion orders and any inaccuracies in the text which result from these or any other changes to the routes nor any damage which might result from walkers trespassing on private property. We are anxious though that all details covering the walks are kept up to date and would therefore welcome information from readers which would be relevant to future editions.

INTRODUCTION

At first glance it might seem the prospects for waterside walking in Sussex are not promising. The landscape of the South Downs is generally dry and there are no large areas of natural inland water in either East or West Sussex; and in recent years, the coastline between Newhaven and Chichester has been extensively developed.

On closer examination, however, it proved much easier to put together 20 walks with a watery theme than I first thought! Along the coast, the harbours at Chichester, Pagham and Rye are designated as nature reserves and are explored on Walks 1, 3 and 20. The remaining unspoilt coastline, between Seaford and Eastbourne and to the east of Hastings, is now well protected from modern developments (Walks 16 and 18). The reservoirs at Ardingly, Arlington and Bewl Bridge, constructed after the date when water authorities were first required by statute to take account of recreational interests, offer three pleasant circuits (Walks 11, 13 and 15).

The rivers of Sussex provide a focus for the majority of the walks on offer. Some of the best walking in Sussex can be found in or near the river valleys of the Arun, Adur and Cuckmere as they carve their way through the South Downs. Upstream from these lower reaches, good riverside walking proved more elusive. The network of public rights of way in Sussex, about 4,000 miles in all, first evolved to provide reliable links between settlements. These routes tended to avoid river banks, picking higher and drier ground, as Walk 2 in the Western Rother valley, delightful and varied though it is, illustrates well. The path from Barcombe Mills to the Anchor Inn on Walk 10 in the upper Ouse valley, does, exceptionally, follow the river for some distance, but floods regularly during the winter months leaving the pub marooned. My chosen river walks each sample at least a short section of the river bank but tend to rise to higher ground to complete the circuit, often providing a fresh and interesting perspective of the river valleys.

All the walks in this book follow recognised rights of way or permissive routes where public access has been agreed. Most of the paths are well established but, bearing in mind the low-lying terrain, you should go well shod, prepared for mud, patches of standing water and even, on Walks 3 and 12, the occasional high tide encroaching on the path. As always when following any described walk, I would recommend having an Ordnance Survey map to hand, useful to provide awareness of the surrounding countryside and essential if you do inadvertently go astray. The 1:50,000 scale Landranger sheets should suffice but the new 1:25,000 Explorer series of maps are perfect for the job.

All the walks are circular and have been planned to start and finish at a point where good parking is available; if, however, you decide to opt for roadside parking please be aware of the needs of local people and farming activities and be careful not to obstruct any exits or entrances. You will also find a pub serving good beer and food either on or within easy reach of each route. I have provided fairly detailed information about these hostelries in the introduction to each walk. In addition, I have given brief details about places of interest close to, or within a short driving distance of, the walk route so that you can plan a full day out if your wish.

Putting this book together during the wet summer of 1998, it sometimes seemed as if there was more water coming out of the sky than on the ground. It was, nevertheless, a great pleasure to produce. When the sun comes out – and often when it doesn't – there is no better place to walk than beside the water. After sampling some or all of these walks, I am sure you will agree.

Ben Perkins

WALK 1

CHICHESTER HARBOUR

Some of the best views across Chichester Harbour are obtained from this walk round the bare Chidham peninsula which juts out towards the main navigation channel from the north. It also passes close to the Nutbourne Marshes Nature Reserve, 900 acres of mud which form an important nesting site for sea birds.

Bosham seen from the Chidham peninsula

Chichester Harbour, with 50 miles of shoreline, has been in use since Roman times when a port was established at Fishbourne. By the 17th century, Dell Quay was the only port, but 100 years later the harbour reached its industrial peak, providing access to the canal system via the Chichester Canal, subsequently disused but now partially restored. Today, the harbour provides a base for thousands of yachts. In 1971 the whole area was designated as an Area of Outstanding Natural Beauty in recognition of its importance as a haven for wild life – nesting birds in the spring and vast flocks of migrants in the autumn and winter. The village of Chidham, where the walk starts and finishes, is a scattered hamlet with a tiny flint-walled church dating from the 13th and 14th century, surmounted by a Victorian belfry with, inside, a notable Saxon font.

The nearby 17th-century pub, the Old House at Home, where the walk starts and finishes, is a free house where you are likely to receive a particularly friendly welcome with excellent food and beer guaranteed. Ringwood Best Bitter and Old Thumper, plus Badger's Dorset Best are always available on hand pump, or you can sample Old House Bitter, a mystery beer of unrevealed origin. Guess where it comes from and you can have a free pint. The food menu, not surprisingly, specialises in fresh fish dishes, much of it locally caught. For a more modest but still generous bar snack, freshly baked baguettes come with a variety of interesting fillings.

Opening hours Monday to Friday are from 11.30 am to 2.30 pm and 6 pm to 11 pm, Saturday from 12 noon to 3 pm and 6 pm to 11 pm and Sunday from 12 noon to 4 pm and 7 pm to 10.30 pm. Food is served on weekdays from 12 noon to 2 pm and 6 pm to 9.30 pm and Sunday from 12 noon to 3.30 pm and 7 pm to 9 pm. Booking is advisable at the weekend. Telephone: 01243 572477.

- **HOW TO GET THERE:** From the Chichester bypass, follow the A259, once the main road to Portsmouth, westwards. After about 4 miles, turn left along Chidham Lane and follow signs to Chidham West and the church.
- **PARKING:** Shortly past the church there is room to park on the verge opposite the Old House at Home pub. You can use the pub's car park while on the walk, if you are a customer, but let someone in the pub know.
- **LENGTH OF THE WALK:** 6 miles. Map: OS Explorer 120 Chichester, South Harting and Selsey (GR 786039).

The Walk

1. From the pub, walk southwards along the lane, rounding a left hand bend. Just short of the church, turn right along a well trodden path which takes you through to another lane. Turn left and, after 350 yards, just short of the entrance on the right to a house called 'Woodstock', turn right along a narrow path which takes you through to another lane. Turn left for just under 300 yards before going right along Harbour Way, a private road but also a public footpath from which you get a glimpse over the harbour to the left.

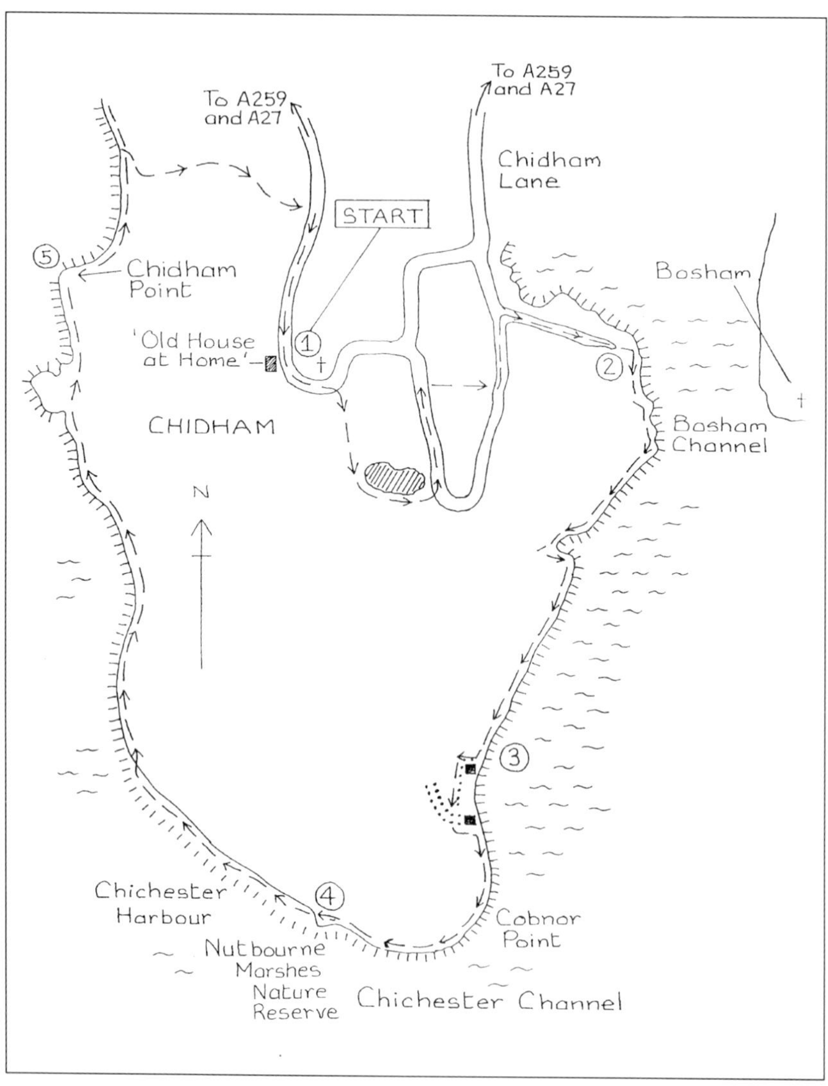

2. Where the road ends at a roundabout, go ahead along a narrow hedged path which takes you out to the water's edge where you should bear right, on the foreshore for a few yards, then on the top of a grassy bank beside the harbour with a succession of fine views across the Bosham Channel to the village of Bosham.

3. After just over a mile, on reaching a wooden pier, the path, well signed, is routed inland, skirting to the right of various buildings, then to the left of a grassy area and through a dinghy park before making its way back to the harbour's edge. From here to Cobnor Point the path has been given a hard surface to make it suitable for wheelchairs. As you round the point you are close to the main Chichester Channel which takes all the main traffic between the Chichester Yacht Basin and the sea, a busy marine thoroughfare. Across the water to the left is West Itchenor, from which a ferry runs to Bosham and back during the summer months.

4. Beyond Cobnor Point, wooden steps take you down onto the shingly foreshore. The path is close to the high water level and you may get wet feet at times of very high tides. Look out for the remains of wooden stakes along the line of an old sea wall, erected in the last century in a vain attempt to reclaim the Thorney Channel from the sea. The whole area, known as the Nutbourne Marshes Nature Reserve, is now protected as a spring nesting site for birds such as redshanks, terns and ringed plovers and, in the autumn a wintering area for waders and wildfowl. After about ½ mile the path climbs back up onto the sea wall, eroded in places. Continue for another mile or so.

5. Shortly after the path and sea wall round Chidham Point look out for a signed path which doubles back to the right and then follows a well trodden headland route out to a lane. Turn right for about 550 yards back to the start.

Places of Interest Nearby

The remains of *Fishbourne Roman Palace*, signposted from the A259, about 3 miles east of Chidham, were uncovered by chance in 1960 during digging operations for a new water main. Now painstakingly excavated, you can see revealed the remains of 20 spectacular mosaic floors, some remarkably complete. The palace garden has been replanted following the original plan. The palace was built in AD 75 and is one of the largest Roman sites in the country. In recent years, further excavations have uncovered evidence of another large building nearby, possibly a military headquarters. Fishbourne Palace is open daily for most of the year. For exact dates and times, telephone: 01243 785859.

WALK 2

THE WESTERN ROTHER: STEDHAM, IPING, CHITHURST AND TROTTON

Four unspoilt villages, four ancient river bridges and four quiet country churches are visited on this varied walk in the valley of the Western Rother.

The River Rother near Stedham Mill

The Western Rother, a main tributary of the River Arun, rises on the other side of the county border near Petersfield in Hampshire. It quickly enters West Sussex, flowing eastwards through a valley sandwiched between the chalk downs to the south and an extensive area of greensand heathland to the north. The river is punctuated by a series of tiny villages each on the site of an ancient river crossing. Although it may not provide much in the way of riverside walking, this is an attractive circuit, never far from the Rother and offering a chance to visit and admire four ancient river bridges at Stedham, Iping, Chithurst and Trotton as well as four village churches.

The Hamilton Arms at Stedham is unusual in that it doubles as a Thai restaurant, but remains very much a genuine village pub, offering a range of good beer, including the local Ballard's Best Bitter, Fuller's London Pride, Thai Elephant beer and a couple of guest ales. The Thai cuisine spills over into the bar in the form of specially prepared Thai bar meals such as fried Thai noodles with shrimps, turnip, peanut, egg and bean sprouts or roast duck with sesame sauce and pickled ginger on rice. There is also a good standard English menu. The pub is open on Tuesdays to Saturdays from 11 am to 3 pm and 6 pm to 11 pm and on Sundays from 12 noon to 3 pm and 7 pm to 10.30 pm. It is closed all day Monday. Food is served daily (except Monday) from 12 noon to 2.30 pm and 6 pm to 10.30 pm. Telephone: 01730 812555.

- **HOW TO GET THERE:** Stedham is signposted from the A272 Midhurst-to-Petersfield road about a mile west of Midhurst.
- **PARKING:** There is no official car park at Stedham but you should find roadside parking space along the north-south village street beside the village green.
- **LENGTH OF THE WALK:** 4½ miles, or 5½ miles including the extension to Trotton Bridge and the nearby church. Map: OS Explorer 133 Haslemere and Petersfield (GR 862223).

THE WALK

1. Start the walk by continuing northwards along the village street which drops down towards the river. About 30 yards short of the attractive low-arched 17th-century Stedham Bridge, turn left along a signposted bridleway, beside the river at first, then across higher ground. Follow this clear path for over ½ mile, finally passing a house on your right. A short cobbled path takes you out to reach the lane at Iping.

2. There are two drives opposite. Take the one on the left but after a few yards, fork right on a narrow enclosed path. Over the next stretch you are never far from the Rother, away to the right, but remain insulated from it. Where the enclosed path ends, go forward along the right edge of two fields and on along another enclosed path to reach Chithurst Lane.

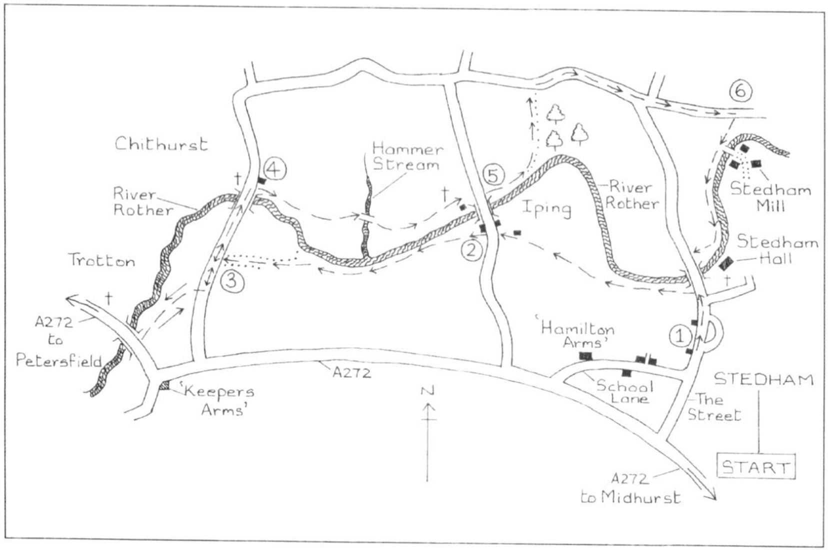

3. You now have a choice. For the shorter walk, turn right and continue along the lane to Chithurst.

To visit the bridge and church at Trotton, turn left and, after about 200 yards, go right on a signed path between fence and hedge. Beyond a stile, head out across a field. Cross another stile and turn left beside a fence, soon veering right, away from the fence, to cross two more stiles, in sight, and a small meadow to reach the A272. Trotton church is now a short distance to the right across the fine 15th-century bridge; the Keeper's Arms pub is equidistant to the left. Inside the church you will find the tomb of Thomas, Lord Camoys, adorned with what has been described by Ian Nairn as one of the biggest, best and most ornate brasses in England. It features Lord Camoys and his second wife, Elizabeth, widow of Harry Percy, Shakespeare's Hotspur. Reverse your steps to point 3 and continue north along the lane.

On both the longer and shorter routes you will cross another fine old bridge over the Rother to reach Chithurst church, a simple, largely unaltered, 11th-century structure set on a mound overlooking the river, a wonderfully atmospheric place.

4. A few yards short of the church, turn right along a roughly metalled track past farm buildings to a stile. Go forward, keeping to the right of a tree-lined bank and a barn to the next stile. Cross the

next field to find and cross an elegant iron footbridge over the Hammer Stream, a tributary of the Rother. Beyond the bridge, turn right to walk round the right hand edge of a large field. Head out across the field beyond to find a stile to the left of a bungalow. Walk out past Iping church, a Victorian building with a rather odd square tower, to join a lane with another fine river bridge a few yards to the right.

5. Go through a gate opposite and follow a faint track along the right hand edge of a large field. The river is once again tantalisingly close on your right but screened by trees. Follow the track as it veers right through a gate but, after a few yards, go left over a stile and continue along the right edge of two fields to join a lane. Turn right. Ignore a 'No Through Road' going back to the left. At a staggered crossroads, go ahead, signposted to Woolbeding.

6. After another 1/4 mile or so, turn sharply right on a wide path which drops down between high wooded banks. At the bottom of the hill where the path comes out into the open, ignore a stile on the left and go forward for a few yards to reach the River Rother, where a bridge above a weir leads to Stedham Mill, providing one way back to the start. For a better route, turn right along the nearside river bank to follow, at last, a genuine riverside path, offering at one point a view across the water of the dramatic stone and half-timbered front of Stedham Hall, a suitable setting for a romantic novel. The path veers right, away from the river, to join a lane. Turn left back to the start. Stedham church, along a lane to the left, is worth the short detour.

Places of Interest Nearby

The small market town of *Midhurst*, 2 miles away down the Rother valley, has developed next to another important river crossing and has many fine old timber framed buildings. Just outside the town, amidst the wide acres of Cowdray Park, is an Elizabethan ruin. A few miles south of Midhurst at Singleton is the *Weald and Downland Open Air Museum*, a fine collection of old buildings saved from demolition or ruin and re-erected on a spacious site. Highlights include a 15th-century Wealden hall and a 14th-century farmhouse. Telephone: 01243 811348.

WALK 3

PAGHAM HARBOUR NATURE RESERVE

If you are likely to encounter a high tide, the best time to fully appreciate the attractions of this marvellous walk on the western side of Pagham Harbour, wear your wellies. Although most of it follows dry raised banks, some sections descend to the foreshore which can be very wet, or even awash, beyond point 3 at times of spring tides. The figure-of-eight form of the walk will allow you to choose different lengths according to weather, time and tide. But whenever, and wherever, you go there will be birds!

Sidlesham Quay

Pagham Harbour, previously known as Udring Haven, was once a flourishing sea port. From here, in 1412, ships and men set sail for Harfleur en route for Agincourt and later, in 1588, to combat the Spanish Armada. The harbour was barraged in 1876 and the whole area reclaimed for agriculture. The sea defences were destroyed by a storm in 1910, leaving the harbour much as it is today, a 700 acre area of saltmarsh and mudflat, providing habitats for a wide variety of birds. In winter comes an invasion of waders and wildfowl including pintails, teals, and thousands of Brent geese. Summer visitors include shelduck and nesting terns, ringed plovers and oystercatchers. As at Rye Harbour (Walk 20), the open water at Ferry Pond (point 2) and Pagham Lagoon on the other side of the harbour act as a magnet for both birds and birdwatchers.

From the main Visitor Centre, our walk offers two loops, both beside the harbour and back across farmland. The first half heads northwards to Sidlesham Quay where there is an excellent pub and the second half south to the hamlet of Church Norton.

The Domesday Book records an ale house on the site of the Crab and Lobster pub although the present building dates from 1720. It stands next to the site of the old Sidlesham Harbour and Tide Mill, once a busy commercial area, now a quiet and beautiful backwater. It is a free house with four real ales on tap at all times, including Fuller's London Pride and Golden Arrow Bitter from the Somerset based Cottage Brewery Company, plus two guest beers. The food menu, as you might expect, specialises in fresh fish dishes such as Selsey crab salad or home made crab cakes, but also includes a good choice of pub favourites. The Crab and Lobster is open on Monday to Saturday from 11 am to 3 pm and 6 pm to 11 pm and on Sunday from 12 noon to 3 pm and 7 pm to 10.30 pm. Food is served daily from 12 noon to 2.15 pm and 7 pm to 9.30 pm except on Sunday evenings. Children under 14 are not allowed in the bar. Telephone: 01243 641233.

- **HOW TO GET THERE:** From the Chichester bypass, take the B2145 Selsey road, passing through the villages of Hunston and Sidlesham. The car park and Visitor Centre are signposted on the left, beyond Sidlesham.
- **PARKING:** There is a large free car park next to the Pagham Harbour Visitor Centre.
- **LENGTH OF THE WALK:** 3 miles (Sidlesham Quay loop only, points 1, 2, 3 and 4), 4½ miles (Church Norton loop only, points 5, 6 and 7) or 7½ miles (full walk). Map: OS Explorer 120 Chichester, South Harting and Selsey (GR 857966).

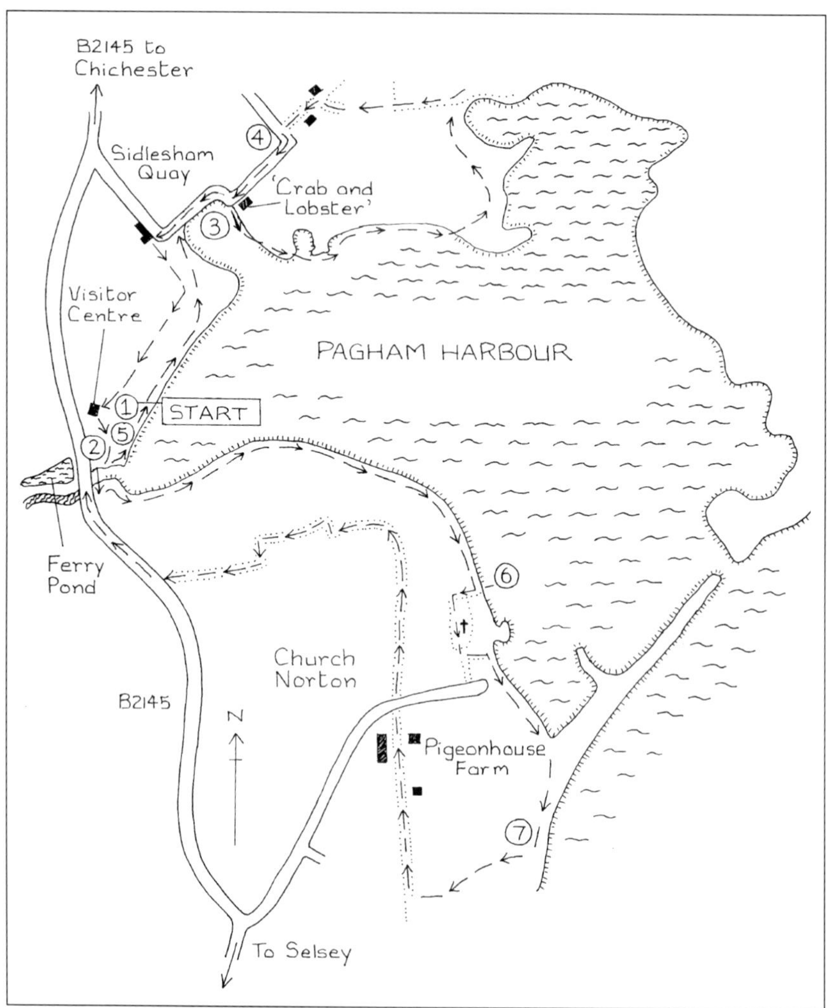

THE WALK

1. Walk out of the car park and turn left past a metal barrier and along a gravel path which is the start of the Sidlesham Ferry Nature Trail, for which a leaflet is available from the Visitor Centre. It is marked with wooden posts and you will be following part of it on the first loop of the walk. Walk past a bird hide on your right, overlooking Ferry Pond. Although separated from the pond by the busy B2145, it is described as one of the best birdwatching spots in Sussex. The birds are clearly less disturbed by cars than people.

The pub near Sidlesham Quay

2. Just past the hide, go through a swing gate and turn left soon on a long, straight track along the western edge of the harbour, once part of the Selsey Tramway. It takes you out to a road where you should turn right, soon passing Sidlesham Quay, once a busy harbour and the site of a tide mill until the harbour was sealed and drained in 1876.

3. Just past the quay, where the lane bends left just short of the Crab and Lobster, go ahead along the harbour edge, passable, though wet in places, except at times of very high tides. Keep close to the wall on your left. Eventually a clear path continues on a slightly raised bank. Beyond a nature reserve notice, go forward along the left edge of two fields, through a gate and ahead along a track. At a junction with another track near Halsey's Farm, turn left out to a lane.

4. Turn left and follow the lane back past the Crab and Lobster to point 3 and on past the point where you joined the lane on your outgoing route. Shortly, where the lane bends round to the right, go left along a rough track to a stile and ahead along the right edge of a field, following the headland round to the right. From the end of the field a path continues along the top of a tree-covered bank.

Steps on the left take you back to the Visitor Centre and the start.

5. For the second leg of the walk, follow the same route (point 1) as far as the swing gate at point 2, beyond which you should go ahead, parallel to the road on your right which is on a causeway replacing the ferry which originally linked the island of Selsey with the mainland. After less than 100 yards, bear left with the path which now follows a raised bank with the main harbour channel and then the extensive saltmarsh of Pagham Harbour to your left. At one point you are obliged to drop down onto the shingle at the edge of the harbour but can soon regain the raised bank.

6. After about 1¼ miles, the path bears right, away from the harbour, and then crosses a wall into Church Norton churchyard. Go forward, passing to the right of St Wilfred's Chapel, the 13th-century chancel of a church demolished in 1864 to provide material for the present church at Selsey. Leave the churchyard through the main lychgate and, after a few yards, turn left along a track which takes you back to the harbour. Turn right and follow the harbour shore and then a raised shingle bank with the sea away to your left.

7. On reaching the first wooden breakwater on your left turn right along a clear path which heads inland. At a signed T-junction turn right and shortly go forward along an access drive. Walk between the buildings at Pigeonhouse Farm and on to join a lane. Turn left and, after 15 yards, go right along a metalled drive which soon becomes a farm track and heads out, unfenced, between large cultivated fields. The track continues between hedges and soon turns squarely left. Follow the track round two more double bends and out to join the B2145 where you should turn right.

This is a busy road but there is a narrow grass verge on the right and then a pavement on the left for most of the way. Just beyond a sharp right hand bend, go right along a signed path. After a few yards turn left, retracing your steps past point 2 and back to the start.

Places of Interest Nearby

The walled cathedral city of *Chichester* should not be missed while you are in the area. The cathedral itself is a magnificent structure with a soaring spire visible for miles.

WALK 4

THE WEY AND ARUN CANAL NEAR LOXWOOD

The Wey and Arun Canal once formed a vital link in a commercial waterway between the River Thames and the South Coast. A partially restored section of the canal provides the focus of this gentle stroll on good level paths and tracks.

Brewhurst Lock

The $18^{1}/_{2}$ mile length of the Wey and Arun Junction Canal, to give it its full title, was opened with a flourish in 1816 when a procession of barges was seen off by two brass bands from Alfold, not far from the start of our walk. The canal was never a commercial success and, finally killed off by the coming of the railway, was closed to traffic in 1871. Now, over 100 years later, the Wey and Arun Canal Trust have undertaken the slow and painstaking task of restoring London's 'lost route to the sea'. Many bridges and 29 locks will need to be replaced, and an adequate water supply restored.

On this walk from Loxwood, we can follow one of the few renovated sections of the canal, passing several elegantly restored bridges and two fully working locks. At weekends during the summer you can take an afternoon trip along a fully functioning section of the canal below Baldwin's Knob Lock aboard the long boat *Zachariah Keppel*, operated by the Wey and Arun Canal Trust.

The 17th-century Onslow Arms, once a bargees' watering hole, is now a flourishing country pub and is passed twice on the full walk. It has a spacious interior and a large beer garden beside the canal and the neighbouring River Lox. The beer on offer comes from the Hall and Woodhouse Badger brewery. You can choose from their Tanglefoot or Golden Champion Ale. The food menu includes most of the pub favourites plus daily specials and a pizza menu with interesting toppings (try the 'Lox' – salmon, prawns and mushrooms – or the 'Bargeman' – spicy beef, mushrooms and peppers). There are bar snacks too, but no sandwiches on Sundays. Opening hours vary, but are normally from 11 am to 3 pm and 5.30 pm to 11 pm on Monday to Friday, from 11 am to 11 pm on Saturday, at least in summer, and from 12 noon to 10.30 pm on Sunday. Food is available from 12 noon to 2 pm and 5.30 pm to 9 pm daily. Telephone: 01403 752452.

- **HOW TO GET THERE:** Loxwood can be reached along the B2133, either from the A281 Guildford-to-Horsham road at Alfold Crossways or, if approaching from the south, from the A272 a mile to the west of Billingshurst.
- **PARKING:** There is limited roadside parking along Station Road which heads east from the B2133 in the centre of the village, or a few yards along estate roads to left and right off Station Road (Nicholsfield and Farm Close). Alternatively, particularly if you are only tackling the shorter walk, the Wey and Arun Canal Trust have a large car park behind the Onslow Arms at point 2. Access is through the pub car park.
- **LENGTH OF THE WALK:** 5 miles, or 3¾ miles if you start and finish at point 2. Map: OS Explorer 134 Crawley and Horsham (GR 038315 – point 1; GR 041311 – point 2).

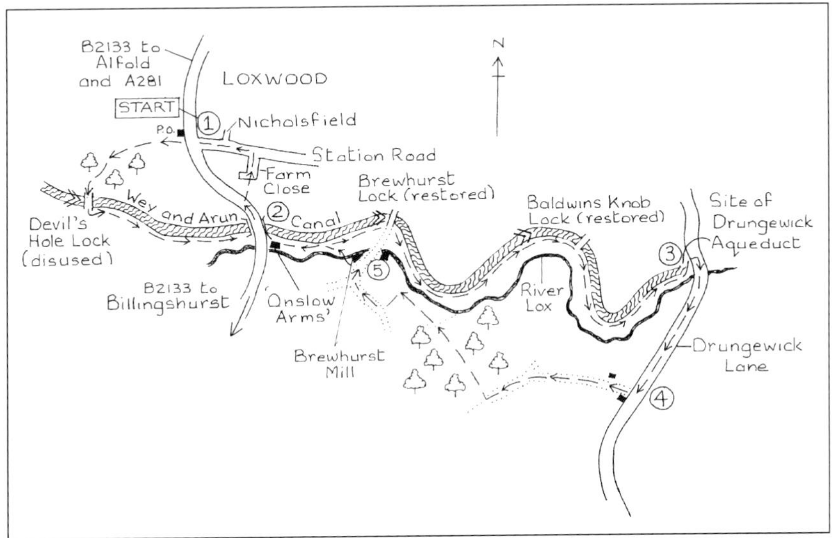

The Walk

1. Return to the road junction with the B2133, cross the road and follow a signed path which starts to the left of Loxwood post office and passes some new cottages, ignoring a bridleway which forks right. Continue along a left field edge and along a pleasant tree-lined path which drops down to join the Wey and Arun Canal next to Devil's Hole Lock, cleared but not yet restored. Cross a fine new brick bridge and turn left beside the canal, dredged but not in water.

2. At the B2133, cross the road, turn right for a few yards and then go left, just short of the Onslow Arms, resuming your walk along the canal towpath and passing the car park which provides your alternative starting point. From here the canal may well be in water, depending on recent rainfall and the level of the feeder river nearby. Walk past Brewhurst Lock, renovated as recently as 1996. Cross a drive beside Brewhurst Bridge and carry on to Baldwin's Knob Lock, restored in 1993. A landing stage below the lock provides the starting point for summer boat trips. At other times you will find the trip boat *Zachariah Keppel* moored along this stretch of the canal, which is kept full of water when necessary by a specially installed pump. The River Lox which supplies water to the canal is to the right, never far away. A milepost tells us that, from this point, it is 14 miles to the River Wey and 9 to the Arun.

3. Where the restored section of the canal comes to an abrupt end, go ahead passing the site of the Drungewick Aqueduct, which once carried the canal across the River Lox and is now on the list for early restoration. Join Drungewick Lane and turn right. Public access is denied to the next section of the canal so we must follow the lane across the Lox and the canal.

4. After 700 yards, turn right along the access drive to Drungewick Kennels, signed as a public bridleway, which soon becomes a wide tree-lined track. After a little over 1/4 mile, at a T-junction, turn left along a roughly metalled track and, after another 200 yards, at a four-arm footpath sign, turn right along a narrow path which passes through open broadleaved woodland and then drops down to follow a tiny stream. Cross a footbridge and, at a junction with a wider track, bear left. Leave the wood and continue on a wide, grassy, fenced path. Beyond another gate, at a junction, turn right along a concrete drive. At another junction, turn right again, still on a metalled drive.

5. Just short of the white weatherboarded Brewhurst Mill, turn left across a brick bridge, noting the old mill wheel on your right. Go over a bridge above a sluice and walk through a meadow to rejoin the canal. Turn left and retrace your steps out to the road by the Onslow Arms, back at point 2. Turn right and after about 60 yards, go right again along a narrow signed footpath with a tarmac surface. On reaching an estate road, go ahead to join Station Road and left, back to the start.

PLACES OF INTEREST NEARBY

Easily within range via Wisborough Green and the A272 are *Petworth House and Park*. The house is one of England's grandest mansions, built using local stone in 1688 on the site of an earlier house. The magnificent west front, 320 feet long, overlooks an extensive deer park in which the public are invited to walk freely. The interior of the house, now looked after by the National Trust, is notable for a Grand Staircase and the elaborate wood-carved decoration of the spectacular Grinling Gibbons Room. It is open April to October every afternoon except Thursday and Friday. Telephone: 01798 342207.

WALK 5

THE ARUN VALLEY: SOUTH STOKE AND ARUNDEL PARK

After a stroll beside Swanbourne Lake and a steady climb across the open grassland of Arundel Park, a sharp descent brings us down into the Arun valley for a delightful riverside walk back to the start. It is possible to link this circuit with Walk 6.

The Arun valley

The Arun is the most substantial river in Sussex and has carved the widest of the three river gaps through the South Downs. This broad and beautiful valley is dominated on the west by Arundel Castle and the heights of Arundel Park. At Swanbourne Lake, visited at the start of the walk, there are rowing boats for hire, water level permitting, and tea rooms at the eastern end of the lake. It is a popular spot for family outings and can get very crowded. At 'off-peak' times and out of season it is a delectable spot.

The 1,200 acres of Arundel Park are part of the Norfolk Estate in which the public are invited to wander freely except on 24th March each year. Dogs, however, are not permitted at any time.

The Black Rabbit pub, which can get very busy, is well placed towards the end of the walk and enjoys a perfect setting, nestling beneath a steep wooded slope, with a terrace and small shady garden overlooking the river. The beer on offer includes Badger's Tanglefoot and Dorset Best plus an exclusive Black Rabbit ale from the local Arundel Brewery. Food is served from a cafeteria style bar with a choice of about half a dozen dishes from the hot plate and a variety of help yourself salads. The opening times on Monday to Saturday are from 11 am to 11 pm and on Sunday from 11 am to 10.30 pm. Food is served all day during the summer, othewise from 12 noon to 3 pm and 6.30 pm to 9 pm daily, though these times may vary according to demand. Telephone: 01903 882828.

- **HOW TO GET THERE:** From the eastern end of the Arundel bypass on the A27 Worthing-to-Chichester road, follow the road towards the town. At the next roundabout, turn right along Mill Road.
- **PARKING:** You can park without charge almost anywhere along the eastern side of Mill Road between the town and Swanbourne Lake. In summer or at weekends, be sure to arrive early to avoid the crowds or you may have to use the pay-and-display Mill Road car park.
- **LENGTH OF THE WALK:** 6 miles. Map: OS Explorer 121 Arundel and Pulborough (GR 019077). This walk can be linked with Walk 6 at South Stoke to provide a figure-of-eight circuit totalling 10½ miles.

The Walk

1. From wherever you managed to find room to park beside Mill Road, carry on along the road, using a path lined by lime trees to the right. Once over a fine stone bridge you should fork left along a path which passes in front of the entrance to a trout feeding pond and continues along the left edge of Swanbourne Lake. At the far end of the lake, double back to the right to follow a wide, roughly metalled track along the other side of the lake.

2. Fairly soon, where the track dips down to round a small inlet, turn left through a gate and walk along the floor of a beautiful dry downland valley, climbing very gently. On reaching a block of

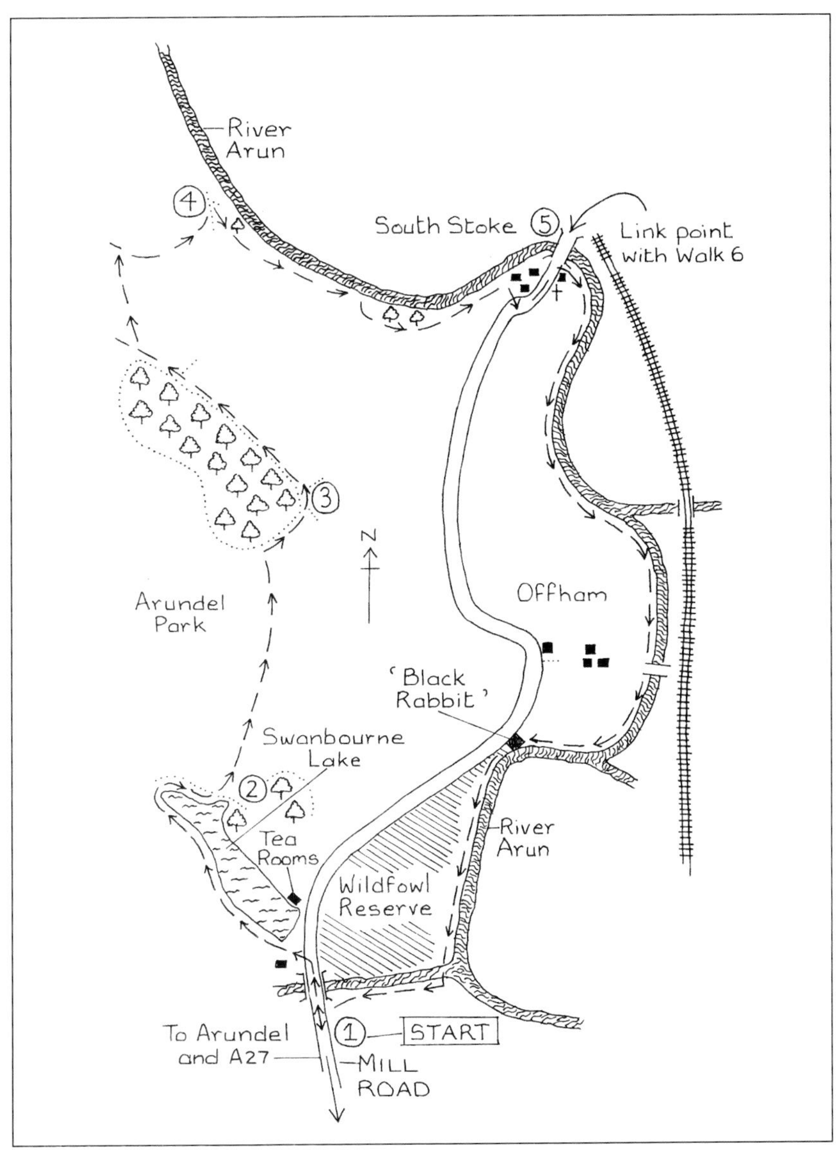

woodland at the head of the valley, bear right along the edge of the wood, now on a clear track which brings you to a gate and a superb view across the Arun valley and back towards Arundel Castle. The church ahead of you in the valley is at South Stoke, visited later in the walk.

3. Immediately beyond the gate, bear left to a second gate and follow a clear track along the rim of the valley with the wood still on your left. After 700 yards, go through another gate and after about 100 yards, veer half right off the track, dropping gently down to another gate leading into a chalk and flint track which drops fairly steeply down into the Arun valley. At a T-junction turn right and after about 100 yards bear left on a narrow path with a fence, right, which takes you down to the bottom of the hill where the path joins and follows the Arundel Park wall to your right.

4. Go through this wall, using a new high iron swing gate, and turn right along a well signed bridleway which follows the river Arun to South Stoke, though concealed from it by a thick bank of trees and scrub. On approaching this tiny hamlet, follow the directions on a sign, turning sharp right and keeping to the right of a rather unusual brick-built Victorian barn with five arches to join a lane. Turn left and, where the lane divides, fork left, soon passing the entrance to South Stoke church on your right. You may find sheep grazing in the churchyard surrounding this lovely little flint church. Beyond the church the lane dwindles to a track and takes you down to a bridge over the River Arun.

5. Don't cross the bridge (which provides the link with Walk 6). Instead, turn right and follow the nearside river bank downstream for 1½ miles to join a lane for a few yards, passing the Black Rabbit pub. Beyond the pub, resume your walk along the river bank with a good view ahead to Arundel Castle. After about 700 yards, go through a swing gate and immediately turn right on a path along the top of a raised bank between reed filled ditches. It brings you out to Mill Road by the stone bridge crossed at the start of the walk.

Places of Interest Nearby

Arundel Castle, the seat of the Dukes of Norfolk, was built in the 11th century, partially destroyed during the Civil War in 1643 and then restored in stages during later centuries. It contains many fine furnishings and paintings and is open from 1st April to the end of October on Sundays to Fridays from 12 noon to 5 pm. Telephone: 01903 882173. Access to the *Arundel Wildfowl and Wetlands Reserve* is from Mill Lane between Swanbourne Lake and the Black Rabbit. Open daily. Telephone: 01903 883355.

WALK 6

THE ARUN VALLEY: BURPHAM AND NORTH STOKE

A riverside and downland walk at the upper end of the Arun gap. Although it can be enjoyed separately, it is possible to link this circuit with Walk 5, extending it downstream and up onto the heights of Arundel Park.

Arundel Park seen from the River Arun

A walk along the banks of the River Arun today provides few clues to its busy industrial past. Navigable in its lower reaches since about 1550, river traffic reached a peak following the opening of the Wey and Arun Canal in 1816, creating a link between the River Thames and the sea. Decline set in rapidly after the railway arrived in 1863 although barge traffic as far upstream as Bury Wharf did not cease until as late as 1929. Today only the trains and an occasional small pleasure boat mar the tranquillity of this lovely river valley. The village of Burpham, where the walk begins and ends, derives its name from the Saxon 'burgh' or fortified township which at one time occupied the plateau to the south of the village, a commanding position overlooking a loop of river, once the main channel of the Arun.

The only other settlement visited on the walk is the tiny hamlet of North Stoke, with a population today of less than 50. The 12th-14th century church, without a patron saint dedication, was made officially redundant in 1992, but is now cared for by the Churches Conservation Trust. The return route climbs onto the low hills on the eastern side of the valley with fine views across to Arundel Park and Castle.

The George and Dragon at Burpham, standing opposite the church, has served as a pub since it was built in 1730. It offers a good range of beers including Harveys Sussex Bitter and Burpham Best from a local Lancing brewery and guest beers, changed weekly. The food menu is an impressive one and includes the usual bar snacks. The opening hours on Monday to Saturday are from 11 am to 2.30 pm and from 6 pm to 11 pm and on Sunday from 12 noon to 3 pm and 7 pm to 10.30 pm. The pub is closed on Sunday evenings in winter. Food is served daily from 12 noon to 2 pm and from 7 pm to 9.45m (9 pm on Sunday). Telephone: 01903 883131.

- **HOW TO GET THERE:** From the A27 Worthing-to-Chichester road just east of Arundel Station, follow a long cul-de-sac for 2½ miles via Warningcamp and Wepham to reach the church and the George and Dragon pub at Burpham.
- **PARKING:** There is a free car park behind the George and Dragon pub, next to the recreation ground.
- **LENGTH OF THE WALK:** 4½ miles. Map: OS Explorer 121 Arundel and Pulborough (GR 039088). This walk can be linked with Walk 5 at South Stoke to provide a figure-of-eight circuit totalling 10½ miles.

THE WALK

1. Walk back to the lane by the George and Dragon and turn left. After a few yards, where the lane bears right, go ahead along a 'No Through Road' which soon narrows to a path. Where the path divides, fork right, soon dropping down to cross a low-lying meadow. Join and follow the raised bank of a redundant loop of the Arun on your left, now a quiet backwater though still connected

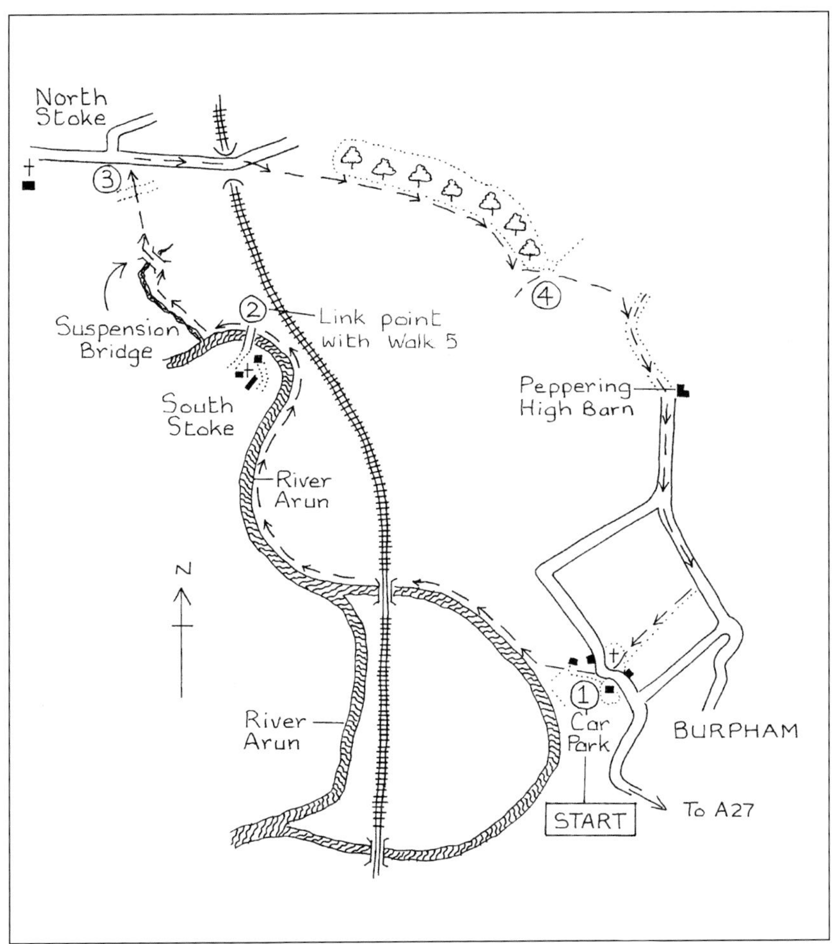

with the main river. Follow the raised floodbank until, soon after crossing the railway, you join the main river channel at the end of a new cut, constructed in 1860 when the railway linking Arundel with Pulborough was being built.

After another ½ mile, the river curves to the left round another horseshoe 'new cut', encircling South Stoke and dug out at an even earlier date in 1839 when improvements were made to the Arun Navigation. A bridge over the river (White Bridge) gives access to the hamlet of South Stoke and it also provides the link with Walk 5. The combined circuits would make a fine day's walking.

2. To complete this walk, do not cross the bridge. Instead, go ahead along the river bank, with the heights of Arundel Park, explored on Walk 5, directly ahead of you. After another 100 yards or so, turn right over a stile and go ahead on a path along a raised shady bank. The ditch on your left is all that remains of the old course of the Arun. The raised path leads to a charming little suspension bridge over the old river and on between fields. Go across a track and continue ahead for a few yards to join a lane.

3. North Stoke church is a few minutes away, along the lane to the left. Return the same way or, if omitting this detour, on reaching the lane, turn right. After almost 400 yards, fork right through a bridle gate beside a farm gate and follow an unfenced track which drops down and continues along the foot of a tree-covered slope rising up to the left.

4. After 2/3 mile, at a meeting of several paths, go ahead over a stile and follow a narrow, fenced path steeply uphill. At the top, turn right along a chalk and flint track with superb views back across the valley and ahead through the river gap at Arundel to the coastal plain. Beyond Peppering High Barn the track becomes a road. At a road junction fork left and after another 270 yards, go right along a headland path which takes you back to Burpham. Once into Burpham churchyard, go ahead, skirting to the left of the church, out to join the lane opposite the George and Dragon pub.

Places of Interest Nearby

The *Amberley Museum*, less than a mile from North Stoke on foot but accessible by road only via Arundel, occupies a 36 acre site in an old chalk pit. It contains a remarkable collection of displays from the world of industrial archaeology, including various craftsmen's workshops, vintage road vehicles, a reconstructed village garage and telephone exchange and many other exhibits. You can ride around the site on a vintage bus or along a narrow gauge railway and there are regular special events during the summer months. The museum is open from 10 am to 5 pm from April to October but is closed during the winter months. Telephone: 01798 831370.

WALK 7

WIGGONHOLT AND PULBOROUGH BROOKS

This is an easy walk, mostly on level ground, offering, in all seasons, the opportunity to observe a variety of wild life, particularly if you decide to add the 2 mile RSPB nature trail to the described circuit.

The River Arun

Upstream from Amberley to Pulborough and beyond, there is almost no public access along the banks of the River Arun so we must make the most of what is available. Although only a small part of this circuit can strictly be described as beside the water, the walk as a whole has a distinctly watery feel about it, as much of it crosses the restored wetlands of Pulborough Brooks. Until 1989, when the Royal Society for the Protection of Birds purchased a large part of the area, drainage improvements had led to a progressive loss of this important wild life habitat. This trend has now been reversed and the Brooks are now an important breeding area for wading birds such as snipe and redshank. The low-lying meadows are grazed by cattle and cut for hay during the summer. Controlled flooding during the winter ensures the presence of large flocks of migrating wildfowl. The higher, drier ground provides winter grazing and the many hedgerows between these grazing areas offer nesting sites for other birds including warblers and nightingales. Armed with a permit from the RSPB Visitor Centre (fee payable, free to RSPB members) you can extend the walk along a 2 mile nature trail, visiting several bird hides en route. The Visitor Centre, housed in a restored barn, incorporates an information display, shop and tea rooms. It is open every day except Christmas Day and Boxing Day from 10 am to 5 pm and the nature trail and bird hides can be visited from 9 am to 9 pm or dusk (telephone: 01798 875851).

The Oddfellow's Arms at Pulborough can be found about halfway round the walk. It has a spacious timbered bar area divided by a large central fireplace open on two sides and a sheltered beer garden at the rear. Beers on draught include Flowers Original, Fuller's London Pride and at least two guest beers. The simple bar snack menu includes soup, sandwiches, ploughman's and filled jacket potatoes as well as a small selection of more substantial main dishes. The pub is open from 11 am to 3 pm and 6.30 pm to 11 pm on Monday and Tuesday, from 11 am to 11 pm on Wednesday to Saturday and from 12 noon to 3 pm and 7 pm to 10.30 pm on Sunday. Food is available daily from 12 noon to 2.30 pm and 7 pm to 9.30 pm. Telephone: 01798 873766.

- **HOW TO GET THERE:** Approaching from Pulborough on the A283 Pulborough-to-Storrington road, about 2 miles south of Pulborough, fork right, along the first of two roads signposted to Greatham and Rackham. If arriving from the Storrington direction it will be the second road signed to Greatham and Rackham.
- **PARKING:** Access to the car park is beneath a height barrier on the right, about 100 yards along this road.
- **LENGTH OF THE WALK:** 4 miles. Map: OS Explorer 121 Arundel and Pulborough (GR 062163).

The Walk

1. From the far end of the car park, start the walk along a path which passes between a row of low wooden posts to the left of a

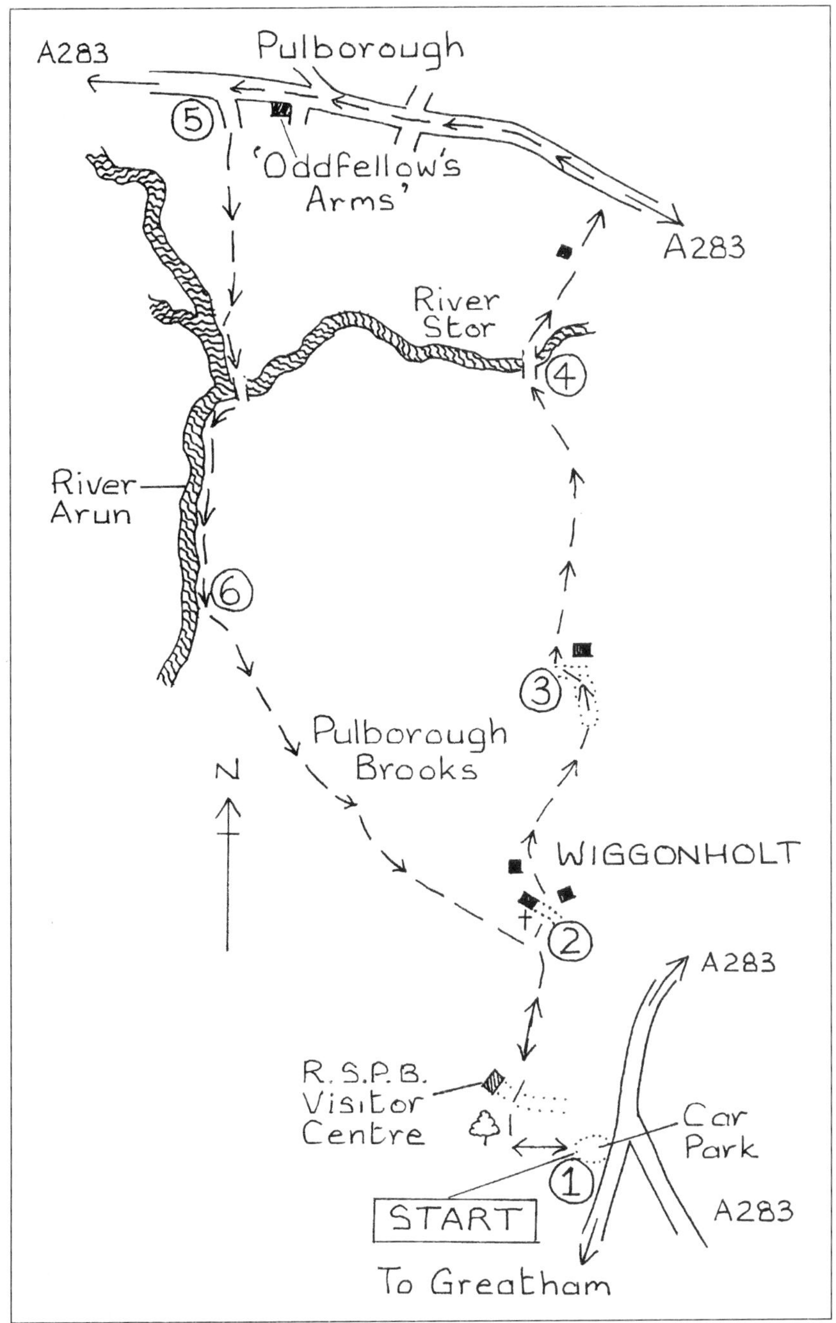
A283
Pulborough
5
'Oddfellow's Arms'
A283
River Stor
4
River Arun
6
3
Pulborough Brooks
N
WIGGONHOLT
2
A283
R.S.P.B. Visitor Centre
Car Park
1
START
A283
To Greatham

Pulborough Brooks

gate and burrows through scrub and bracken. Where the path divides, fork right, skirting to the right of the RSPB Visitor Centre car park. Cross the concrete drive to the Visitor Centre and go forward on a signed footpath.

2. After about 300 yards, cross a drive, leaving Wiggonholt church and the gateway to the Old Rectory on your left. Go over another stile and bear left with the walled garden of the Old Rectory now on your left. Keep to the left edge of two fields. In the second field corner join and go forward on a roughly metalled track.

3. After about 100 yards, turn left on a path which drops down through scrub and bracken to a stile. Go forward to a second stile and onward, skirting to the left of a cottage. Beyond another stile, ignore a right fork and continue on a grassy path along the right edge of the valley with Pulborough Brooks spread out to your left.

4. Go over a footbridge and forward with a stream and then a fence on your right. Beyond a stile an enclosed path leads via an access drive up to the A283. Turn left into Pulborough.

5. After $1/4$ mile, soon after passing the Oddfellow's Arms on your left and opposite the village post office on the right, turn left down Barn House Lane. Where the lane ends, go ahead over a stile and descend onto Pulborough Brooks. Pick up and follow a rife, the local term for a drainage channel, and stay with it to join the Arun river bank which you can now follow downstream, soon bearing right across a bridge over a side stream and continuing beside the river to enter a Countryside Stewardship area.

6. After just under $1/2$ mile, go through two squeeze stiles and after another 150 yards, fork left off the raised river bank and along a faint grassy path across the brooks to a stile beside a gate. The path now bears left and climbs to higher ground. Go straight over a crossing track, part of the RSPB nature trail, over a stile beside a gate and ahead across a meadow to another stile/gate combination. Bear half left, go over two more stiles by gates and follow a clear track up past the tiny 12th-century Wiggonholt church on your left.

Like North Stoke church, further down the Arun valley and visited on Walk 6, it is not dedicated to any specific patron saint. It was built for the shepherds who worked on Pulborough Brooks but, unlike North Stoke church, it has not been made redundant and there are services at least twice a month.

Just past the church you will find yourself back at point 2 where you should turn right along the fenced path used at the start of the walk. Reverse your steps back past the RSPB Visitor Centre to the start.

Places of Interest Nearby

About a mile south along the A283 is the entrance to *Parham*, a superb Elizabethan mansion, beautifully situated in spacious parkland overlooked by the northern escarpment of the South Downs. Built in 1577, it is notable for a spectacular Long Gallery and houses a fine collection of furniture and paintings. The house and seven acre garden are open from April to October on Wednesday, Thursday and Sunday afternoon. Telephone: 01903 742021.

WALK 8

THE UPPER ADUR: SHERMANBURY AND WINEHAM

The quiet upper reaches of the River Adur provide the focus for this peaceful riverside walk from Mock Bridge to Wineham, returning along the disused back drive to Shermanbury Place.

The River Adur

The River Adur derives its name from a 17th-century topographical description of England, penned in verse by a certain Michael Drayton, who was under the false impression that Shoreham, at the mouth of the river, was the Roman *Portus Adurni*. The river is formed from two main tributary streams rising near West Grinstead and Wineham respectively. Public access to one of these tributaries has, in recent years, been greatly improved following the diversion of a public footpath and the opening up of another section of river bank under the Countryside Stewardship Scheme as a permissive route which will remain in being at least until the year 2002. It is a delightful walk beside this modest, gently flowing river.

A minor detour at the start of the return route allows us a visit to the Royal Oak at Wineham, one of the few completely unspoilt pubs left in the county. The building, 600 years old, has housed a pub for the last 300. Set back from the road and fronted by a spacious beer garden, it offers a particularly warm welcome to walkers. The interior has all the traditional attributes of the ideal English pub, an uncarpeted flagstone and wood-boarded floor, plain bench seats, a beamed ceiling and an open fire in winter. The beer, Harveys Sussex Bitter and Marston's Pedigree, comes straight from the barrel and the food does not dominate, being confined to sandwiches, plain or toasted, plus ploughman's at lunchtime from Monday to Friday, and a home made soup in winter. The pub is open from 11 am to 2.30 pm and 5.30 pm to 11 pm on Monday to Saturday and from 12 noon to 3.00 pm and 7.00 pm to 10.30 pm on Sunday. Food is served during opening hours. Telephone: 01444 881252.

- **HOW TO GET THERE:** Follow the A281 south from Horsham or north from Henfield. The start of the walk is just to the south of the Adur crossing at Mock Bridge.
- **PARKING:** Along a loop of old road, now a picnic site, segregated from the A281 by trees and accessible beneath low height barriers.
- **LENGTH OF THE WALK:** 5½ miles. Map: OS Explorer 122 (previously 17) South Downs Way – Steyning to Newhaven (GR 212180).

THE WALK

Note: Parts of the walk route are liable to flooding after winter rains, so go well shod.

1. From the parking area, head north beside the A281. Opposite the Bull pub, turn right over a stile and footbridge, bear half left across a meadow to another stile and go forward along a left field edge. In the field corner go over a third stile and head across a field to the next stile with the Adur away to your left. On the other side of the field, cross a stile and sleeper bridge and go forward for 60 yards.

2. Where you have a choice of signed paths go directly ahead, ignoring the path to the left which will provide your return route. On the far side of the field, go ahead with trees on your right. In the field corner go through a gate and on for a few yards before turning

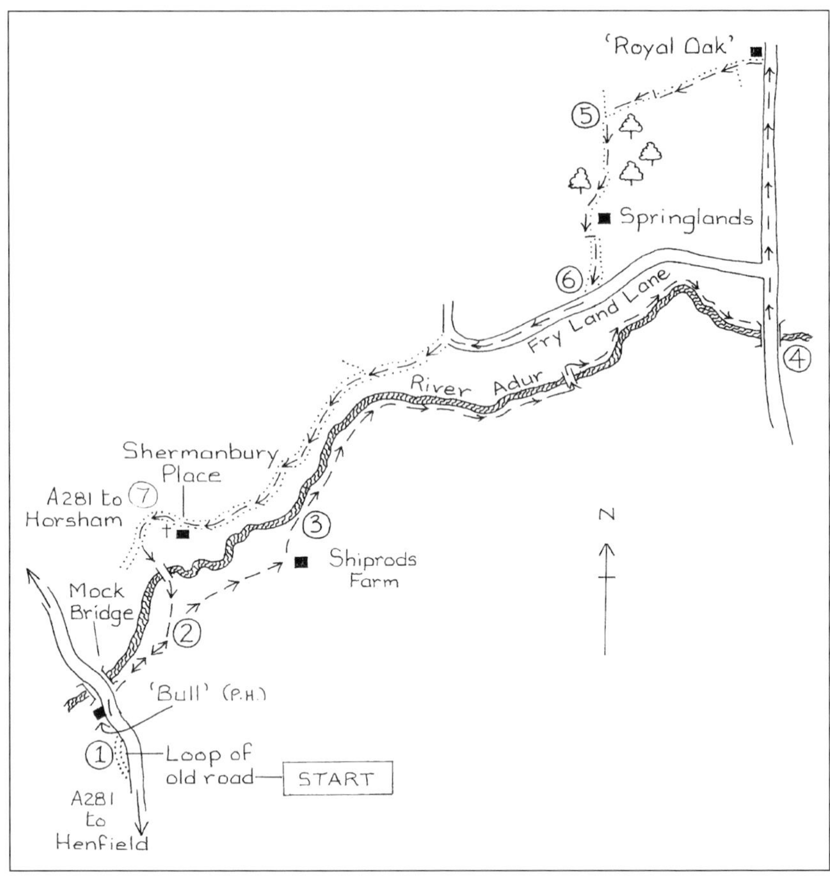

left with the farmhouse at Shiprods with its fine Horsham stone roof across a lawn to your right. A well trodden path (mown at the time of writing) leads to a stile and footbridge over the outlet stream from a pond, then on across rough pastures. A path continues between fence and hedge and then bears left out to reach the River Adur.

3. Turn right along the nearside river bank and follow this beautiful stretch of river upstream. After about 3/4 mile turn left on a signposted path which crosses a bridge over the Adur above a small weir. On the other side turn right along the river bank, now on a path, indicated by white arrows on a green base. It takes you beside the river for another 1/2 mile or so out to join Wineham Lane.

4. Turn left along the lane for a little over 1/2 mile. About 60 yards short of the Royal Oak pub, turn left along an enclosed path, soon ignoring a stiled path to the right. Where the enclosed path ends at another stile, go forward along a right field edge. Just after passing under power lines, sidestep to the right through a gate and resume your previous direction on the other side of the hedge. In the field corner, go over a stile, bear right to a gate and go ahead along a left field edge with trees on your left.

5. In the next field corner go left over a stile and forward, ignoring a second stile on your right. A delightful grassy path between wood and hedge heads south. After about 200 yards, go left over a grass covered culvert, right over a stile and continue southwards along a right field edge. Just short of the field corner go right over a stile, through a wood to a second stile and then left to pass through a gap and skirt to the right of the house, garden and pond at Springlands. Just past a barn on your left, go through another gap and left along a field edge to join the drive from Springlands. Turn right to follow it out to a lane.

6. Turn right along the lane. Where the lane turns to the right, go left over a cattle grid and along a drive, signed as a private road but also as a public bridleway. After about 350 yards, fork left off the drive along a fenced track, once metalled but now reverting to grass. Ignore the first signed path to the left and continue along the main track, passing, on the left, the 18th-century Shermanbury Place and the church of St Giles, a modest structure with a timber belltower. Inside, the box pews bear the names of the local farms.

7. After another 200 yards or so, turn left along a path which starts between white gate posts. Cross the Adur and veer half right across a meadow back to the path junction at point 2. Turn right and retrace your steps to the start.

Places of Interest Nearby

A few miles to the north along the Horsham road are *Leonardslee Gardens*. The gardens are open daily from April to October. Telephone: 01403 891212.

WALK 9

THE LOWER ADUR: BRAMBER AND BOTOLPHS

This relatively short riverside walk should allow plenty of time for minor diversions to three ancient churches and the short climb up to Bramber Castle overlooking the river valley.

Bramber village

From the quiet upper reaches of the Adur, explored on Walk 8, we move downstream to Bramber, where the river, now tidal, carves a gap in the South Downs as it approaches the sea at Shoreham. At Bramber, where the walk starts and finishes, stand the remains of Bramber Castle, built by William de Braose, one of William the Conqueror's knights, soon after the Norman Conquest, but destroyed (like Bodiam – Walk 17) by Parliamentarians during the Civil War. It is now reduced to a scanty, but atmospheric ruin, dominated by a large fragment of wall, standing up above the village like a broken tooth. The church, tucked beneath the castle, was built as the castle chapel at about the same time and also suffered under Cromwell. Only the nave and tower survived but they have been reshaped to form an intimate and harmonious whole.

During the walk, minor detours will allow you to visit two more delightful Sussex churches. The church at Upper Beeding, built in 1073, also by William de Braose, was once the chapel of a Benedictine priory and is notable for a Norman tower. On the isolated site of a 'lost' village in the middle of the Adur valley and within yards of our route, stands the even older Saxon church at Botolphs. It was founded where the route of the 'tin road', linking the tin mines of Cornwall with the Roman port at Pevensey, crossed the river by a bridge, now long gone.

To nourish body as well as mind and soul, there are three pubs on or within yards of the walk, two beside Upper Beeding Bridge and the Castle Inn at Bramber, opposite the start of the walk. The flower-bedecked Castle Inn is large and busy, with a sheltered garden at the rear. It is a free house serving Hancock's HB, IPA and Bass on draught. The food menu is extensive and embraces several inventive vegetarian dishes, as well as a range of bar snacks. The opening hours are long – 11 am to 11 pm on weekdays and 12 noon to 10.30 pm on Sundays – with food available from 12 noon to 2 pm and 7 pm to 9.30 pm on weekdays and through the afternoon as well on Sundays. Telephone: 01903 812102.

- **HOW TO GET THERE:** From the large Shoreham interchange on the A27 west of Brighton, follow the A283 northwards along the Adur valley. Bramber is accessible from a roundabout on the Steyning-Bramber-Upper Beeding bypass.
- **PARKING:** Park in the main village car park at Bramber to the north of the village street almost opposite the Castle Inn.
- **LENGTH OF THE WALK:** 4 miles, not including detours to castle and churches. Map: OS Explorer 122 (previously 17) South Downs Way – Steyning to Newhaven (GR 188106).

THE WALK

1. From the entrance to the car park, turn right along the road, now much quieter since the bypass was opened and traffic calming measures introduced. After a few yards, access to Bramber church and the castle is on the right. At the bypass roundabout, turn right

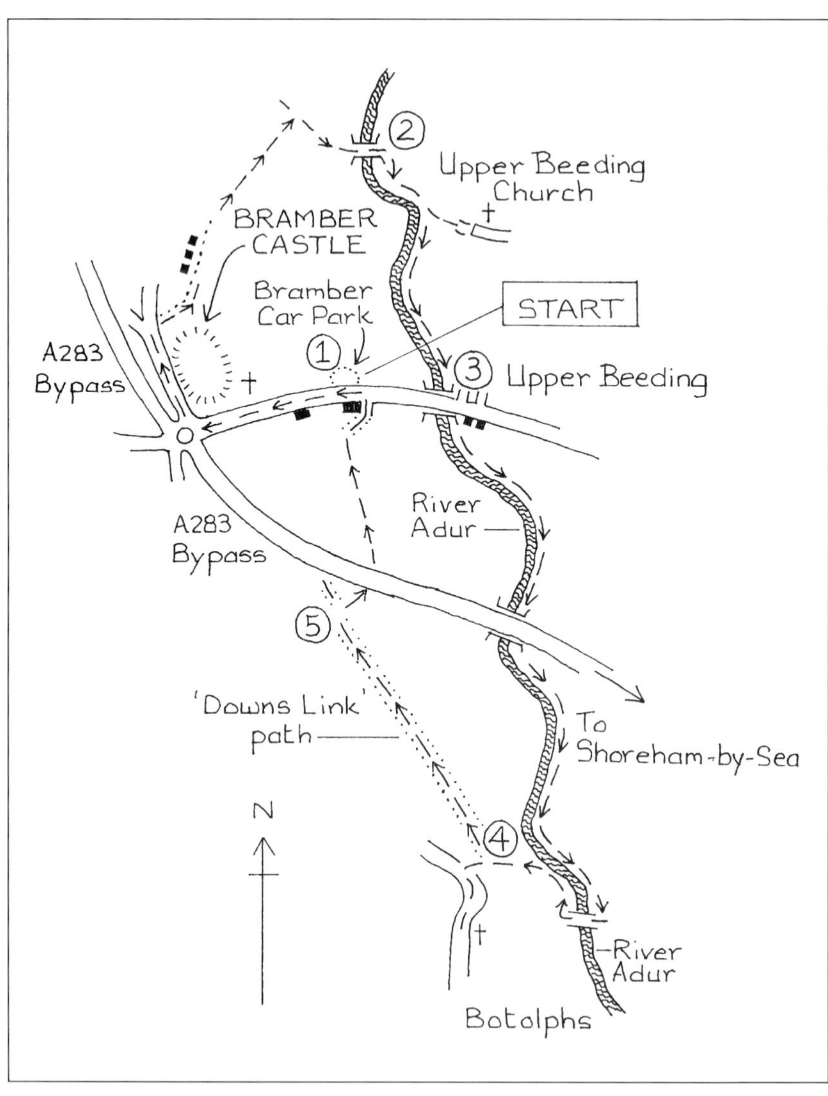

along Castle Lane. After about 300 yards, just short of a road junction, turn right along a rough track which skirts beneath Bramber Castle on the wooded mound to your right. Where the track divides, fork left on a clear path. Ignore a signed path to the left and shortly go forward along the top of a raised bank with a rife (drainage channel) to your right. After about 250 yards, turn right and cross a water meadow to reach the River Adur.

2. Cross a bridge over the river and turn right to follow the raised river bank downstream. Shortly a path to the left provides access to Upper Beeding church, a few minutes walk away. Return by the same route and resume the walk downstream beside the river.

3. Cross the road at Beeding Bridge and continue downstream along the east river bank, passing the beer gardens of two well placed pubs. Walk under the bypass and continue for a little over ½ mile until you can turn right across the river using the South Downs Way bridle bridge. Now go right again upstream beside the river where the path acquires a hard surface to accommodate cyclists using the Downs Link, a long distance route from the coast to Guildford, mainly along the old railway track bed. After 100 yards it veers left, away from the river.

4. After another 100 yards or so, the track divides again, and the walk continues along the Downs Link to the right. If you have time, follow the South Downs Way to the left out to a lane and go left for the short distance to Botolphs church. Return the same way and resume your walk along the Downs Link.

5. After about ½ mile, the track bears round to the right. After 5 yards, where the Downs Link goes off to the left, you should go forward with a ditch on your right. Shortly, cross the bypass, using two stiles. You now have a choice of trodden paths across a large field. Fork left. On the other side of the field, cross a stile and bear right along a fenced track. Cross a stile, then after a few yards go left over a second stile and turn right, rejoining the track which takes you out for the last few yards to the road at Bramber. Turn left, past St Mary's House, back to the start.

PLACES OF INTEREST NEARBY

St Mary's House, Bramber was originally donated to the Knights Templars in the 13th century but most of the present half timbered structure dates from the 15th and 16th centuries. House and garden are open from Easter Sunday to the end of September on Sundays, Thursdays and Bank Holiday Mondays from 2 pm to 6 pm. Telephone: 01903 816205. The nearby village of *Steyning*, once, like Bramber, an important sea port, contains a wealth of ancient buildings, and is well worth a visit.

WALK 10

BARCOMBE MILLS AND THE RIVER OUSE

The first part of this splendid walk is along the bank of the River Ouse to the north of Lewes and provides one of the most attractive riverside walks in the county. The return route departs from the water's edge to follow an old droveway and the track bed of a disused railway.

The River Ouse, north of Barcombe Mills

The River Ouse rises in St Leonard's Forest, near Horsham, and meanders eastwards and southwards before carving a passage through the Downs at Lewes to reach the sea at Newhaven. The river is tidal as far north as Barcombe Mills where our walk sets out along one of the most scenic stretches of the river bank. Barcombe Mills was once a thriving industrial site with a busy flour mill which subsequently became a button factory until it burnt down in 1939. The mill was served by horse-drawn barges, hauled up the river from Lewes, as well as a branch of the railway. It is now a tranquil spot, reserved for walkers and anglers, where the river divides to cascade down a weir, through sluice gates, over fish ladders and into a trout fishing pool. Although controlled by automatic sluices, the river floods easily after winter rain, leaving the Anchor Inn marooned for days at a time. So for winter walking, do check with the Anchor before setting out (telephone: 01273 400414).

You will come to the Anchor Inn after the first mile at point 3, which, as well as the usual pub refreshment, also offers rowing boats for hire and an open air tea and ice cream kiosk during the summer months. Built in 1790, the pub originally catered for barges until the coming of the railways led to the end of river traffic. The railway, too, is now disused though there is some talk of re-opening the Lewes-to-Uckfield link. The Anchor Inn is a freehouse offering three beers on hand pump – Harveys Sussex Bitter, Badgers Best and Tanglefoot. There is also an impressive wine list reflecting the fact that the new pub owners also operate a wine merchant's business, Longford Wines, from the premises. As well as a large restaurant menu, supplemented by daily blackboard 'specials', the bar snacks on offer include baguettes and sandwiches with a choice of 10 fillings and a home-made soup of the day. Puddings include the locally invented banoffee pie and treacle tart. The pub opening times are 11 am to 11 pm on weekdays and 12 noon to 10.30 pm on Sundays. Food is served from 12 noon to 3 pm and 6 pm to 9 pm daily. Telephone: 01273 400414.

- **HOW TO GET THERE:** From the A26 Lewes-to-Uckfield road, about 3 miles north of Lewes, turn off westwards, signposted to Barcombe.
- **PARKING:** The Environment Agency car park is on the right, after a little over ½ mile along the Barcombe road. It is normally open only during the summer months. If closed, there is room to park beside the road further on, near the Angler's Rest pub, joining the walk after point 6.
- **LENGTH OF THE WALK:** 4½ miles. Map: OS Explorer 122 (previously 17) South Downs Way – Steyning to Newhaven or OS Explorer 123 (previously 16) South Downs Way – Newhaven to Eastbourne (GR 435146).

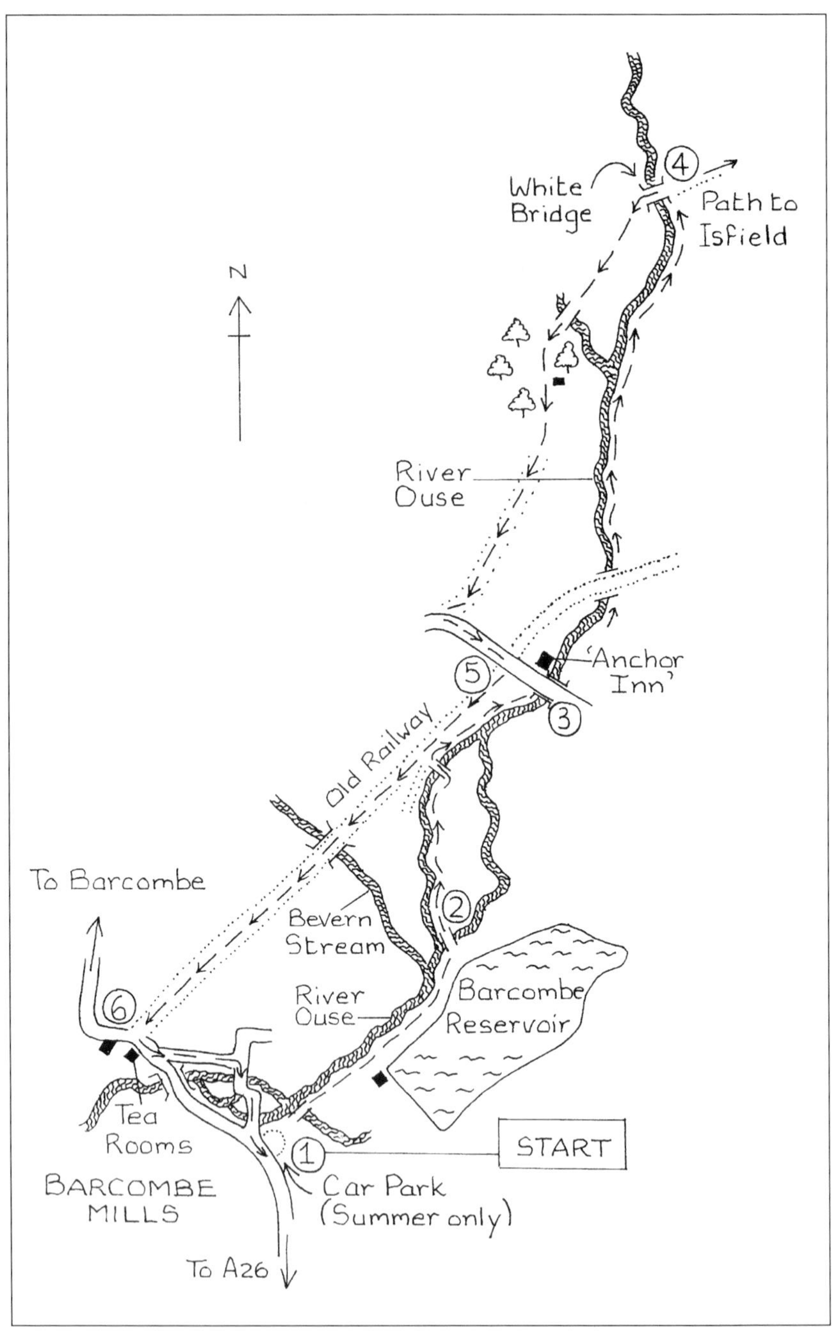

4
White Bridge
Path to Isfield
N
River Ouse
'Anchor Inn'
5
3
Old Railway
2
To Barcombe
Bevern Stream
River Ouse
Barcombe Reservoir
6
Tea Rooms
BARCOMBE MILLS
1
START
Car Park (Summer only)
To A26

Swans nesting beside Longford Stream

The Walk

1. From the entrance to the car park, turn right along the road and, after a few yards, fork right along a roughly metalled track, signed as a 'No Through Road'. After another 100 yards or so, turn right through a squeeze stile and, after a further 200 yards, bear left over a footbridge across the drainage channel from the Barcombe Reservoir. A path now heads upstream along the river bank, soon with the raised grassy embankment of the reservoir to your right.

2. After about 600 yards, go left over a second side stream and continue with the river on your left, narrow and overhung with trees as it meanders between lush meadows. Follow the river bank until you can go left over a wide concrete bridge and right along a drive. After less than 100 yards, fork left along a path which winds through trees and passes to the left of a white weatherboarded house before rejoining the Ouse, now on your right.

3. On reaching the Anchor Inn, turn right, back across the river, and go left along the other bank. Continue upstream through meadows. For part of the way you are crossing Countryside Stewardship land to which open public access is granted.

4. After about $^2/_3$ mile, turn left over the river once more (White Bridge) and, beyond a bridle gate, go half left across a large meadow. Cross another bridge over the Longford Stream, a minor tributary of the Ouse. Shortly after leaving the shelter of some trees, fork left (almost straight on). Pass two oak trees and the upturned stump of a third and keep to the right of a pill box, one of many built in the area during World War II to defend the valley in the event of an invasion. Go forward past four more trees in line and on along a well ridden grassy strip between widely spaced hedges, probably an old droveway. Follow it out to a lane and turn left.

5. After 200 yards or so, turn right along the track bed of the old railway which operated from 1858 to 1967. It is now signposted as a licensed path to Barcombe Mills and provides easy walking. It is wide enough to have developed as a haven for wildflowers, reasonably insulated from the herbicides which have been applied to the fields on either side, and brings you out to a lane opposite the old Barcombe Mills station site, now converted to tea rooms, florist's and gift shop.

6. Turn left along the road and, within a few yards, fork left along a path which continues as a lane. At a junction with the entrance to Barcombe House in front of you, turn right past the old Toll House where the tariff list is still posted. A series of bridges carry the track over and past the pools and sluices constructed to serve the original mill, and out to the lane within yards of the car park.

PLACES OF INTEREST NEARBY

At the *Bentley Wildfowl and Motor Museum*, about 3 miles to the east, you can enjoy the somewhat incongruous combination of vintage and veteran motor cars and various wildfowl including black swans, flamingoes and a variety of ducks and geese. This family attraction is open daily from April to September and at weekends during the winter. Telephone: 01825 840573. The old station at Isfield, a mile to the north, has been restored and operates steam trains along a short section of the old Lewes-to-Uckfield railway, now known as the *Lavender Line*. Telephone: 01825 750515.

WALK 11

ARDINGLY RESERVOIR

After a 2 mile stroll along the water's edge, this walk climbs over higher ground before dropping down through woodland to cross a finger of water at the remote northern tip of the reservoir. We return via Ardingly church where an optional extension, 1/2 mile each way, allows a visit to the Oak Inn in Ardingly village.

Ardingly Reservoir

Ardingly Reservoir was constructed and first flooded in 1978. The damming of the Shell and Ardingly Brooks, both feeder streams of the River Ouse, gives the reservoir its interesting bifurcated shape, straddling two small valleys, on the southern slopes of a well wooded sandstone ridge at the western end of the High Weald. When full, the reservoir is 45 feet deep and holds almost 5,000 million gallons – or 15,908 million coke cans as a South East Water leaflet helpfully explains! Disappointingly, the public are restricted to less than half of the 6 mile perimeter of the reservoir but this walk makes the most of the access available.

On the return route, you will be passing close to the South of England Showground, so avoid the days of the big shows if you want peace and quiet. On the other hand you could easily combine the walk with a visit to a showground event, avoiding major traffic and parking problems.

The Oak Inn, $1/2$ mile off the route from point 6, is a lovely old pub with a compact beamed interior incorporating a bar area and a small restaurant. It also has an attractive garden. Harveys Sussex Bitter and Badger's Tanglefoot are always available on draught. The extensive food menu includes favourites such as steak and Guinness pie plus changing 'blackboard specials'. For snacks you can choose from sandwiches and jacket potatoes with a wide variety of fillings. Opening hours are 11.30 am to 2.30 pm and 5.30 pm to 11 pm on Monday to Thursday, 11 am to 11 pm on Friday and Saturday and 11 am to 10.30 pm on Sunday. Telephone: 01444 892224.

- **HOW TO GET THERE:** From Haywards Heath, follow the B2112 northwards, forking left along an unclassified road (High Beech Lane), signposted to Ardingly. The access road to the reservoir is to the left, about a mile south of Ardingly village. An alternative would be to catch a bus from Haywards Heath to Ardingly, $1/2$ mile off the route of the walk.
- **PARKING:** There is a large free car park at the foot of the reservoir dam. If you would like to start from Ardingly village, you can park in the Oak Inn car park as long as you let someone know and, of course, patronise the pub.
- **LENGTH OF THE WALK:** 5 miles. Map: OS Explorer 135 (previously 18) Ashdown Forest (GR 336287).

THE WALK

1. From the car park, set off past a useful information notice, walk up to the top of the reservoir dam and turn right along it. At the end of the dam, turn left along the reservoir perimeter path. At the start you will be following part of the waymarked 'Kingfisher Trail'. A path on the left leads to a hide from which, if you are lucky, you may be able to spot the eponymous bird as well as many other species. Follow the main path beside the water for almost $1/2$ mile to join a road and turn left to cross a causeway separating two segments of reservoir.

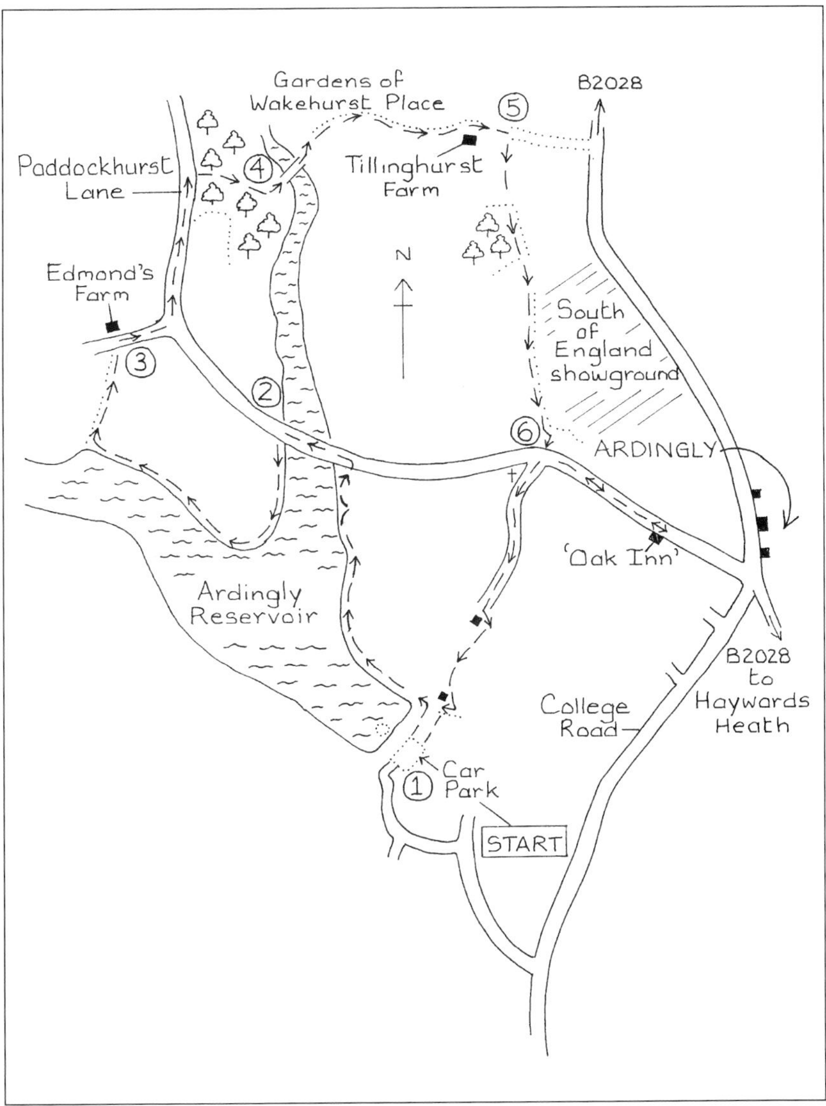

2. At the other end of this causeway, turn left and rejoin the perimeter path which you can now follow for another ½ mile or so. About 100 paces beyond another bird hide at the end of a wooden jetty, turn right through a bridle gate and keep to the left of two fields, climbing gently out of the valley to join a lane in front of

The Oak Inn, Ardingly

Edmond's Farm, a fine timber framed building with a roof of Horsham stone.

3. Turn right and, at a road junction, go left along Paddockhurst Lane. After a little under a $\frac{1}{4}$ mile, turn right past a log barrier and follow a clear woodland path which leads you down to a footbridge across a finger of water at the northern end of the reservoir. Gates to the right on both sides of the bridge lead into the Loder Valley Nature Reserve, which might provide an interesting extension to the main walk. You will need a permit to enter, obtainable in advance from The Administrator, Wakehurst Place, Ardingly, RH17 6TN.

4. To continue the main walk, open at all times, cross the bridge and bear left along a track. Shortly, go right over a stile and climb, with the perimeter fence of Wakehurst Place on your left. The path becomes a track which skirts to the left of the buildings at Tillinghurst Farm. Go forward along the metalled access drive from the farm.

5. After about 200 yards, turn right along a fenced grassy strip, then continue within the edge of woodland and forward along, or on the grass beside, a wide concrete road with the South of England Showground on your left. After 500 yards, where the showground fence veers left, go with it, but after a few yards, turn right through a bridle gate and follow a short metalled drive out to a lane. The Oak Inn is now just under ½ mile along the road to the left, returning the same way. If starting from Ardingly village or the pub, pick up the walk description here.

6. The walk continues to the right. After a few yards, with Ardingly church in front of you, fork left along Church Lane which soon loses its tarmac surface and continues as a rough access track. At the point where the drive opens out into a farmyard, turn sharply left over a stile and walk downhill with a house and garden immediately on your right, ignoring a more obvious mown path across the field. After about 150 yards, go right over a stile and resume your previous direction, dropping downhill along a left field edge with a view of the reservoir to your right.

Beyond another stile, a narrow path winds through a small area of woodland and continues downhill along another left field edge, with the reservoir dam now in view. Where the hedge on your left turns away to the left, go ahead across the middle of a field, dropping down to the bottom left field corner where you will join a metalled drive. Turn right and after less than 100 yards, go left on a path which takes you straight back to the car park, now within sight.

PLACES OF INTEREST NEARBY

The National Trust garden and extensive woodland at *Wakehurst Place* contain many rare species collected together and managed by the Royal Botanic Gardens at Kew. If you visit in the spring, the acid soil ensures a spectacular display of azaleas and rhododendrons. Open every day, except Christmas and New Year's Day. Access is from the B2028 to the north of Ardingly. Telephone: 01444 894066.

WALK 12

THE LOWER CUCKMERE VALLEY

This is a walk of exceptional variety and richness, starting from Hindover Hill, marked on maps as 'High and Over', a magnificent viewpoint overlooking the meanders of the Cuckmere River. After a sharp descent it follows the river to Exceat and then climbs to higher ground on the other side of the valley, returning via the villages of Westdean and Litlington.

The meanders of the Cuckmere

In its lower tidal reaches, the Cuckmere River meanders gently through a wide gap in the Sussex Downs, opening out to an estuary which forms the only major break in the high chalk cliffs of the 'Heritage Coast' between Seaford and Eastbourne. We sample two sections of the river bank, but, if time and energy allow, it is easy to extend the riverside walk either upstream to the village of Alfriston, or downriver to the sea within the Seven Sisters Country Park. To complete the circuit, our walk uses paths on both sides of the valley and visits the villages of Litlington and Westdean. The latter is an enchanting spot, tucked away in a downland hollow, surrounded by trees. It has no pub or shop and is well insulated from the bustling nearby tourist 'honey pot' of Exceat. It has an attractive church with an unusual tower. The Old Rectory, next door, originates from 1220 and, although much restored, lays claim to be the oldest inhabited rectory in the country.

There are two pubs on the route, at Exceat Bridge and Litlington, as well as tea rooms at Exceat. The Golden Galleon at Exceat Bridge is a large and well organised eating and drinking establishment, but is still very much a pub with the emphasis on the variety and quality of the beer. It always has ten real ales on tap, seven from the hand pump and three straight from the barrel. Ales are also brewed on the premises, including Cuckmere Best Bitter, a stronger 'Golden Peace' ale (5.5%) and an excellent stout. Opening hours are 11 am to 11 pm on Monday to Saturday and 12 noon to 10.30 pm on Sunday. An extensive hot food menu is served from 12 noon to 2 pm and 6 pm to 9 pm, with a limited menu including salads and ploughman's available all day, and morning coffee from about 10 am onwards. Telephone: 01323 892247.

- **HOW TO GET THERE:** High and Over is on the unclassified road linking the A27 via Alfriston with the A259 coastal road at Seaford.
- **PARKING:** The High and Over car park is at the highest point on the road about halfway between Alfriston and Seaford.
- **LENGTH OF THE WALK:** 4½ miles. Map: OS Explorer 123 (previously 16) South Downs Way – Newhaven to Eastbourne (GR 509011).

The Walk

1. From the back of the High and Over car park, make your way out through scrub to the end of a bluff with a superb view across the Cuckmere valley. Walk past a direction indicator plate and a National Trust notice, 'Frog Firle', to a stile, from which you should go ahead, signposted to Exceat Bridge. The path drops steeply down and continues out to reach the raised bank of the Cuckmere River.

2. Turn right and follow the river downstream. You will encounter no difficulties except, possibly, at times of high spring tides when the water may encroach on the path and you will have to detour onto higher ground. When your way forward is barred by a fence,

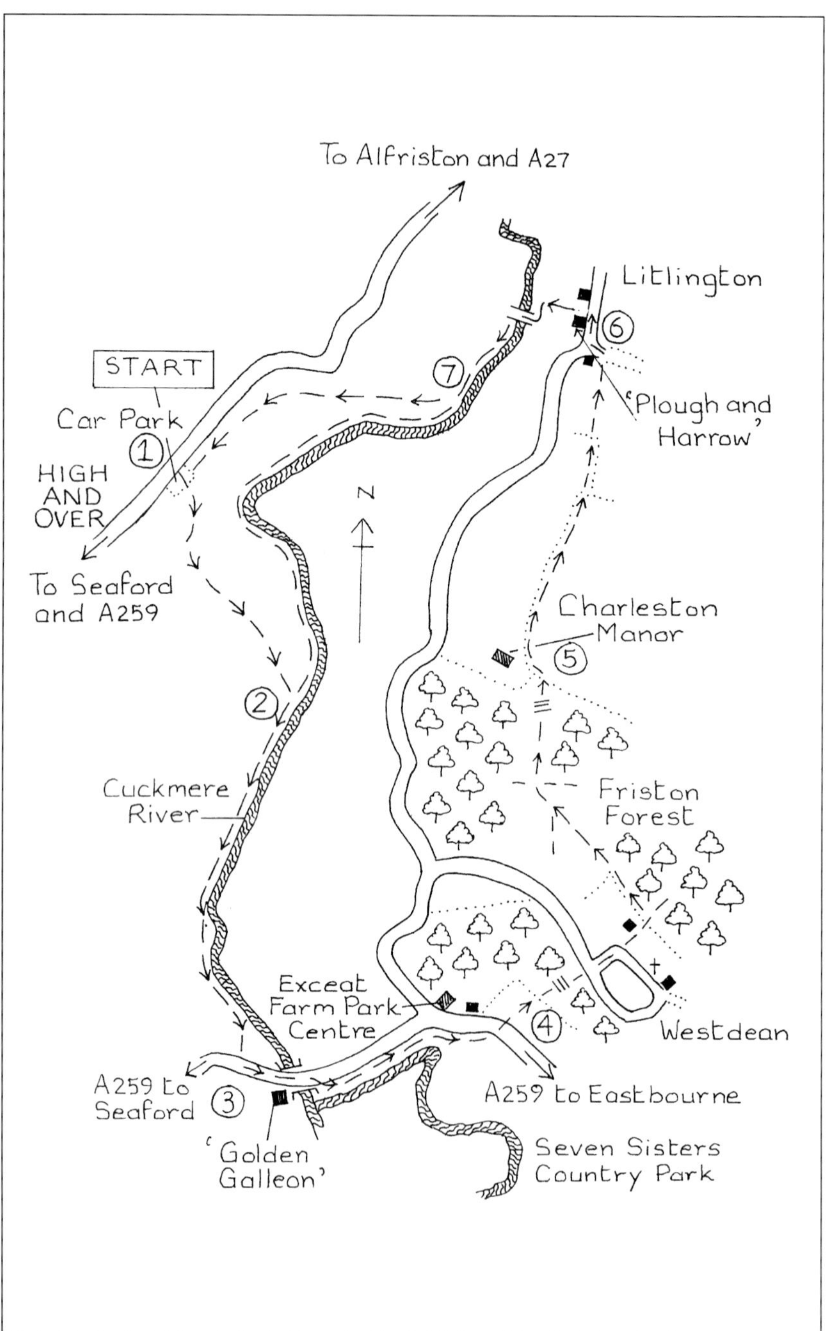
To Alfriston and A27
Litlington
6
START
Car Park
7
1
HIGH
AND
OVER
'Plough and
Harrow'
N
To Seaford
and A259
Charleston
Manor
5
2
Cuckmere
River
Friston
Forest
Exceat
Farm Park
Centre
4
Westdean
A259 to
Seaford
3
A259 to Eastbourne
'Golden
Galleon'
Seven Sisters
Country Park

Litlington village

bear right on a narrow path through scrub out to the A259.

3. Turn left and follow the A259 past the Golden Galleon pub, across Exceat Bridge and on along a raised path beside the road. Cross the road at the bus stop opposite the Exceat Farm Park Centre and follow the South Downs Way which passes to the right of a cycle hire shed. Go through a gate and climb gently up a grassy slope. At the top, where there are a couple of well placed seats, pause to look back across the giant meanders of the Cuckmere, bypassed by a straight new cut between Exceat Bridge and the sea, constructed in 1846.

4. Go ahead over a flint wall and descend a flight of elaborate steps through woodland to reach Westdean village. At the bottom go forward past the village pond, signposted to Litlington. Where the lane bends to the right, go ahead along a concrete drive. From here to Litlington you will be following the South Downs Way, well signed using the familiar acorn symbol. It soon enters Friston Forest, bearing left. Ignore side paths and, after just under ½ mile, go over a crossing path and descend more steps into Charleston Bottom.

5. At the bottom of the hill, bear left and, fairly shortly, turn right over a stile and climb along a clear headland path. Towards the top, there are good views to the left across to the scrub-covered slopes of High and Over. The white horse cut in the hillside is not an ancient hill figure but a fairly modern artefact. In the field corner, go forward over a stile and keep to the right of the next field with Alfriston in view ahead. Go through a kissing gate where you can pick out the spires of Litlington, Alfriston and Berwick churches in almost direct line ahead. A grassy path continues down to join a drive where you should turn left for a few yards out to join the road at Litlington.

6. Turn right past the Plough and Harrow pub. A few yards past the inn, go left along a tarmac twitten. At a path junction, bear left and shortly right to cross the Cuckmere. On the other side of the river, go left along the river bank, re-entering the National Trust Frog Firle estate.

7. Beyond the next stile you have a choice. If you would prefer to pursue the waterside theme, follow the river for a mile, back to point 2, and then turn right, straight up the hill back to the start. For an alternative and very attractive route, which also has the merit of an easier gradient, fork right immediately past the stile where there is a waypost. Cross a hummocky grass area to a second waypost and then climb steadily up a broad grassy spur. Beyond a gate, go ahead, aiming for a second gate on the skyline. Don't go through this gate. Instead, just short of it, bear left and continue to climb, walking parallel to a fence and road to your right. Beyond a stile, a clear path continues up through scrub to the summit of High and Over and the start of the walk.

Places of Interest Nearby

The village of *Alfriston*, although too popular for its own good, is well worth a visit, particularly out of season. The solid cruciform church stands on a low mound overlooking the Cuckmere River and the village green with, nearby, a thatched 14th-century clergy house. *Drusillas Park*, to the north of Alfriston, is an excellent centre for a family day out, incorporating an adventure playground, a miniature railway and a small zoo. It is open every day of the year except Christmas Eve, Christmas Day and Boxing Day. Telephone: 01323 870234.

WALK 13

ARLINGTON RESERVOIR

This walk across level terrain in the upper Cuckmere valley starts with an easy stroll beside Arlington Reservoir and then uses field paths to visit the tiny hamlet of Arlington where there is a convenient pub. After following the Cuckmere River bank for a short distance the walk returns along the top of the reservoir dam.

Cuckmere River

The reservoir at Arlington was constructed in 1971 to tap and store water from the Cuckmere River. Although relatively small as reservoirs go, it has been extensively developed both for anglers and as a nature reserve to encourage the large numbers of wildfowl which congregate here during the winter months. It is also noted as a winter feeding area for osprey. At the north-eastern corner there is a bird hide and a well maintained trail has been laid out round the 2 mile perimeter, much of which is incorporated on our circuit. The walk also visits the village which gives the reservoir its name and includes a short walk along the banks of the Cuckmere, little more than a substantial stream, only a few miles from its source near Heathfield.

The isolated village of Arlington, although almost in the shadow of the reservoir dam, is an unspoilt and peaceful spot, well away from the main tourist routes. The interesting church, Saxon in origin, has been embellished in a hotch potch of styles from the 13th to 15th centuries and even incorporates some Roman fragments.

The Yew Tree Inn at Arlington welcomes you with a spectacular floral display in the summer months. Inside, you can eat and drink in the plain bare-boarded public bar, the comfortable lounge or a bright conservatory opening out into a beer garden at the rear. Harveys Sussex Bitter is on draught and the extensive food menu, all home cooked, is supplemented by daily blackboard specials and includes some rich and interesting puddings. Pub snacks are restricted to ploughman's. The pub is open on weekdays from 11 am to 3 pm and 6 pm to 11 pm and on Sundays from 12 noon to 10.30 pm. Food is served every day from 12 noon to 2 pm and from 6 pm to 9 pm (all day on Sundays). Telephone: 01323 870590.

- **HOW TO GET THERE:** From the Drusillas roundabout on the A27 Lewes-to-Eastbourne road about 3 miles west of Polegate, head north along an unclassified road, signposted to Upper Dicker. Arlington Reservoir is on the right after about 1½ miles.
- **PARKING:** In the large Arlington Reservoir car park, signposted from the road.
- **LENGTH OF THE WALK:** 5 miles. Map: OS Explorer 123 (previously 16) South Downs Way – Newhaven to Eastbourne (GR 528075).

THE WALK

1. From the back of the car park, walk towards the water and after 60 yards turn left along the signed reservoir perimeter path with a fence on your right. The path climbs to slightly raised ground created by spoil excavated during construction of the reservoir but now completely integrated into the landscape. Where the path divides, keep left (almost straight on) along a bridleway which soon leaves the reservoir area and continues along the left edge of two fields. In the second field, veer right with the headland, ignoring an iron gate in the hedge. Pass through a gap into a third field and keep to the left field edge once again. Cross a farm track, go forward over a footbridge to a T-junction of paths and turn right.

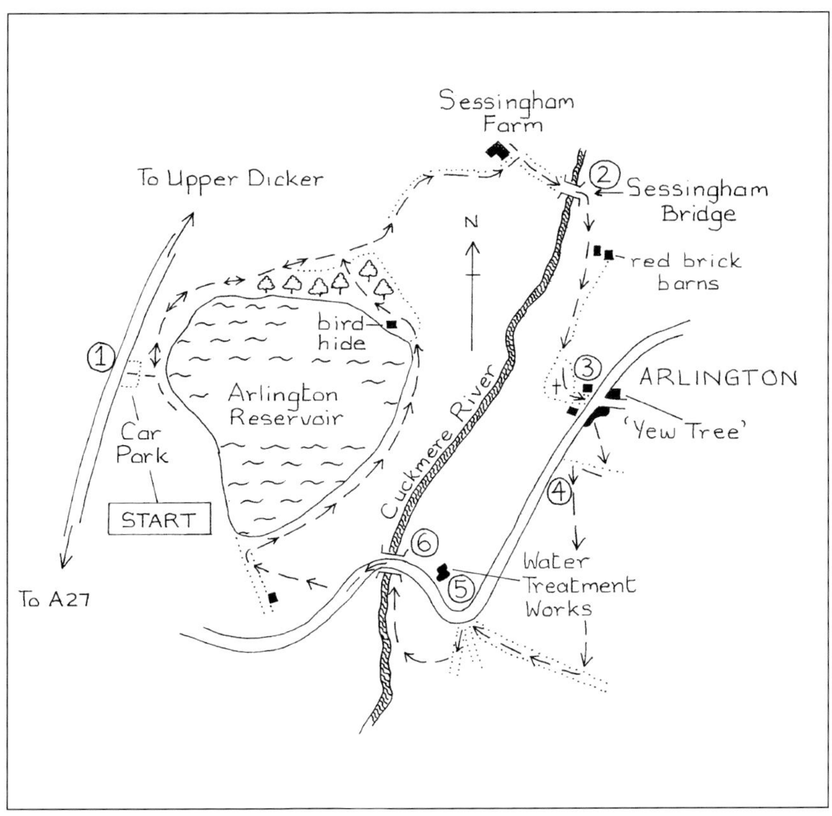

2. Cross the Cuckmere River at Sessingham Bridge and after another 40 yards go right over a stile, adorned with the 'WW' logo of the Wealdway. Cross a field to a stile to the right of two red brick barns and then aim for the spire of Arlington church, converging on and following a hedge, left, with a sweeping view southwards to the Downs. In the field corner go forward over a stile and, after 10 yards, left over a second stile and across a field corner to enter Arlington churchyard.

3. Leave the churchyard through the main gate and turn left. Walk out to the road by the Yew Tree Inn. Your next path starts almost opposite the pub, marked by a yellow arrow. A short green strip between houses takes you out into a field. Head straight out across this field where a path is normally marked out through any growing crop. On the other side of the field go over two stiles and turn sharply right along a right field edge. In the field corner go over a stile and footbridge and ahead with a hedge and ditch on your right.

4. After another 100 yards or so, double back to the left through a bridle gate and cross a meadow to a stile within sight, then the corner of a paddock to the next stile and on in the same direction, obliquely across a field where the path should be clear even if crops have been planted. Maintain direction across two more fields with a stile between them to join a track over another stile and turn right.

5. Where this track joins a drive, just short of a lane, turn squarely left across the drive and go ahead on a grassy hedged track which begins to descend gently. Cross the first stile and just short of a second stile at the bottom of a dip, turn right over a third stile and go forward with a hedge and subsequently the Cuckmere on your left, bearing right along the river bank to join a road.

6. Turn left and after about 250 yards go right over a stile and follow the left edge of rough pasture. Beyond two more stiles, maintain direction across two more fields to join a drive and turn right. Shortly turn right through a gate and walk along the top of the reservoir dam with good views south to the steep scarp slope of the Downs at Windover Hill on which you can pick out the shape of the ancient hill figure of the Long Man of Wilmington. On the other side of the dam go forward through scrub, where a path on the left provides access to the reservoir bird hide. Rejoin your outgoing route and follow it back to the start.

Places of Interest Nearby

Michelham Priory, a moated mansion about 2 miles to the north, upstream along the Cuckmere, is notable for a fine gatehouse and the remains of a 13th-century Augustinian priory. It is open to the public during the summer months. Telephone: 01323 811265. *Charleston Farmhouse*, a few miles along the A27 in the Lewes direction, was once the home of Bloomsbury Group members Vanessa Bell and Duncan Grant. It is open from April to October, Wednesday to Sunday and Bank Holiday Mondays, 2 pm to 5 pm. Telephone: 01323 811265. You can also see murals painted by Grant and Bell in the church at *Berwick*, to the south.

WALK 14

THE MEDWAY IN SUSSEX

From Ashurst on the Sussex-Kent border, this walk explores a quiet stretch of the River Medway, near its source and little more than a stream. The route keeps to the river bank where rights of way permit and also uses a new section of riverside path opened up for public access under the Countryside Stewardship Scheme.

The River Medway

The River Medway is very much a Kentish river but it rises in Sussex not far from East Grinstead and meanders eastwards for 13 miles or so, interrupted by the Weir Wood Reservoir, before crossing the Kent-Sussex border at Ashurst where our walk begins and ends. Public access to the river in these upper reaches is generally poor but a footpath diversion and the opening up of a new permissive path have improved the situation and the link paths used to complete the circuit, across higher ground on both sides of the valley, are attractive enough in their own right and offer excellent views. The walk samples part of two long-distance paths which converge in the area. The Wealdway, 80 miles in length, links Gravesend with Beachy Head while the Sussex Border Path follows the northern Sussex border for 150 miles from Emsworth to Rye.

The Bald Faced Stag pub at the start and finish of the walk offers a warm welcome to walkers. It has a traditional interior and a pleasant sheltered beer garden at the rear. There are usually, at least during the summer months, six real ales on offer. Harveys Sussex Bitter and Bass on draught are supplemented by the pub's own Bald Faced Stag Bitter, brewed at Lancing in West Sussex, and rotating guest beers. The food menu includes the usual bar snacks and a variety of more substantial dishes, including home made curries. The substantial puddings include ramblers' favourites such as spotted dick and jam roly poly. The pub is open from 12 noon to 3 pm and 6 pm to 11 pm on Monday to Saturday and from 12 noon to 3 pm and 7 pm to 10.30 pm on Sunday. Food is normally served during opening hours except on Monday evenings. Telephone: 01892 740321.

- **HOW TO GET THERE:** Ashurst is on the A264 Tunbridge Wells-to-East Grinstead road about 5 miles west of Tunbridge Wells. There is an hourly weekday train service to Ashurst on the Uckfield-to-Oxted line (also a very infrequent Sunday service).
- **PARKING:** At Ashurst Station or at the start of the station approach road, next to the Bald Faced Stag pub.
- **LENGTH OF THE WALK:** 4½ miles. Map: OS Explorer 135 (previously 18) Ashdown Forest (GR 507388).

The Walk

1. Return to the A264 and turn left. A few yards past the start of an access road to houses on your left, you should turn left along a narrow fenced path which squeezes between gardens, passes under the railway and then crosses the River Medway just upstream from a weir and a large pool. On the other side of the river turn left to follow a path, rather overgrown in places, along the river bank.

2. After almost ½ mile, just beyond a stile beside a gate, you should part company with the Medway and veer half right across the middle of a large field where a path is normally marked out through any growing crop. On the other side of the field go through a wide gap in a hedge and turn left to follow the left edge of the next field

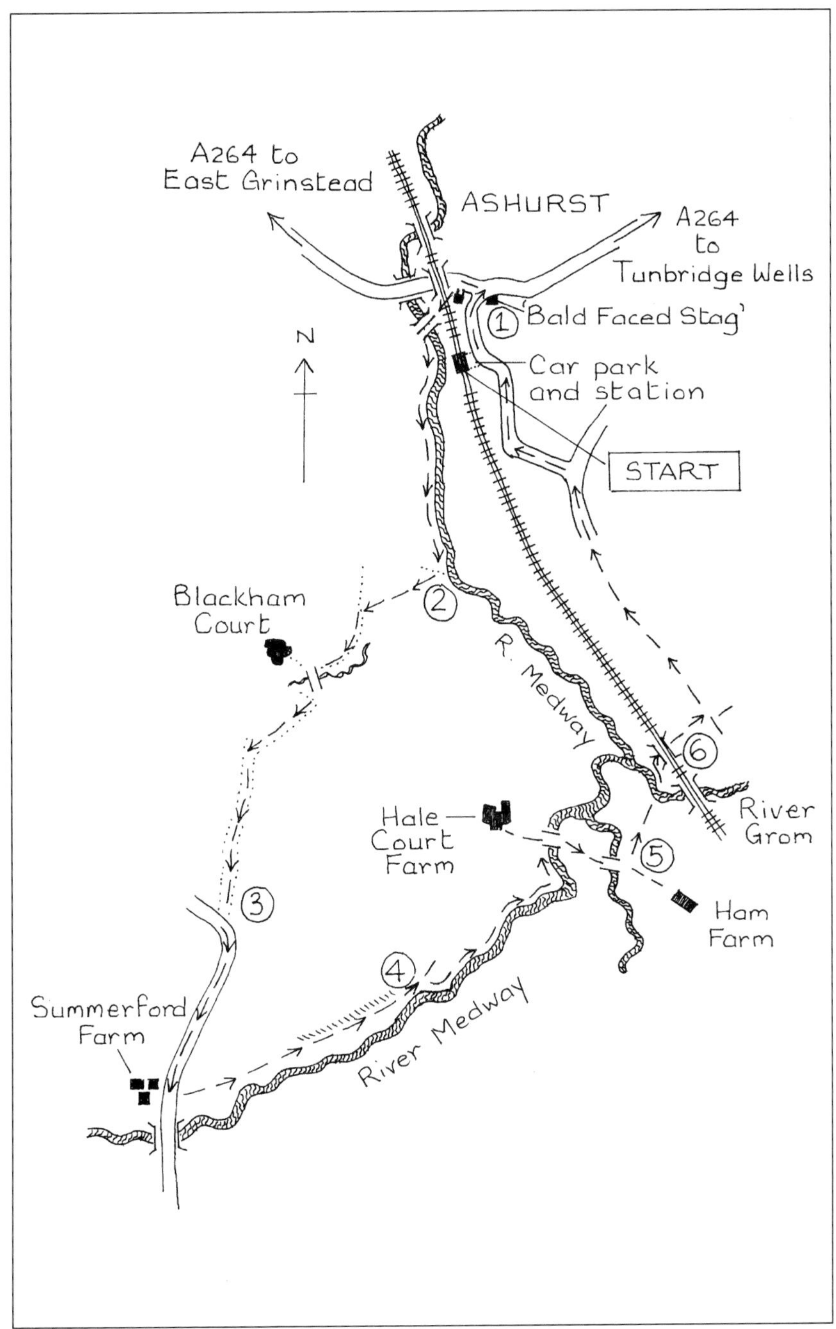
A264 to
East Grinstead
ASHURST
A264
to
Tunbridge Wells
'Bald Faced Stag'
N
Car park
and station
START
Blackham
Court
R. Medway
River
Grom
Hale
Court
Farm
Ham
Farm
Summerford
Farm
River Medway
1
2
3
4
5
6

Jessup's Farm and the Medway valley

as it curves right, soon with a deep ditch on your left. Where this headland path veers right towards the buildings at Blackham Court, you should turn left across the ditch, using a rather dilapidated footbridge. Go straight across the next field to a stile and climb gently out of the valley along the left edge of two fields. On reaching a concrete drive, turn right and follow it out to a lane.

3. Turn left, soon dropping down between high shady banks back into the Medway valley. At the bottom of the hill, turn left over a stile, signposted to Ham Farm and also as part of the Wealdway. Follow the left edge of a meadow, with the Medway to the right on the other side of the field. River and path converge for a while and then diverge again as the Wealdway continues along the meadow parallel to a steep scrub-covered bank on the left. On approaching the field corner, bear left over a footbridge to a stile and walk through a small area of scrub.

4. On emerging from the thicket where there is a Countryside Stewardship notice, turn right to follow the river bank, using a permissive path along a wide headland which is being preserved to encourage wild life including a possible return of the otter which

has been driven almost to extinction in Sussex but is now being sighted again in one or two places. Where the permissive path ends, double back to the right over a concrete bridge across the Medway and follow a wide unfenced track.

5. Immediately beyond another concrete bridge over a tributary of the Medway, where there is a substantial wooden post indicating the meeting point of the Wealdway and the Sussex Border Path, turn left to follow a well trodden strip across a field. Go over another footbridge, erected by volunteers in memory of a local rambler, and continue on a clear path to a white gate and a bridge under the railway.

6. Go forward for about 200 yards to reach another wooden waypost where you should turn left, parting company with the Wealdway but still on the Sussex Border Path. A grassy track climbs gently, soon with good views across the Medway valley towards the distant heights of Ashdown Forest. After about ⅔ mile, turn left along another track which descends between grassy banks. Just short of a red brick cottage (Jessup's Farm) turn right and follow an access track back to Ashurst Station.

Places of Interest Nearby

Groombridge Place, accessible from the A264, a mile to the east of Ashurst, has been developed over the last few years into a major family leisure attraction. The moated Restoration house is not open to the public but you can wander round various small gardens including a sculpture garden, an oriental garden and the Draughtsman's Lawn which featured in the Peter Greenaway film *The Draughtsman's Contract*. The nearby woodland has been laid out as an 'Enchanted Forest'. Open daily from 10 am to 6 pm. Telephone: 01892 863999. The spa town of *Royal Tunbridge Wells* with its elegant central pedestrian area, the Pantiles, developed round one of the original chalybeate springs, is only a few miles away.

WALK 15

BEWL WATER

From the bustling High Wealden village of Wadhurst, this delightful walk descends to follow the shoreline of the Bewl Bridge Reservoir. After almost 3 miles beside the water, the return route crosses undulating, well wooded countryside with superb views.

Bewl Water

The Bewl Bridge Reservoir, or Bewl Water, to give it the less functional label now in general use, is, at 770 acres, the largest area of inland water in South East England. With a 15 mile perimeter and a maximum capacity of nearly 7,000 million gallons, the statistics are certainly impressive. Since its completion over 20 years ago, the reservoir and shoreline have matured into an important wild life habitat. Although excluded from one designated nature reserve, the public have reasonable access to much of the water's edge along good paths and the walk makes the most of this asset. Bewl Water has also been developed as a trout fishery, and you will find the water dotted with anglers' boats during the summer fishing season.

The substantial village of Wadhurst, where the walk begins and ends, is an excellent centre for walks in the High Weald and offers most facilities. The Greyhound is a large, busy pub, well placed in the centre of the village, next to the start of the walk. The building dates from 1502 and gained a reputation as a centre for local smugglers. As a pub it has strong cricketing connections (Maurice Tait, the Kent player, was landlord for a time). Three regular beers are on offer, Bass, Young's Special, and Harveys Sussex Ale, as well as a guest beer. Twelve different wines are available by the glass. The food is all home made and there is a regularly changed blackboard menu of main dishes as well as a wide range of bar snacks, including a substantial 'breakfast roll' (bacon, sausage, mushrooms and tomatoes in a crusty roll). The pub is open from 11 am to 2.30 pm and 6 pm to 11 pm on Monday to Friday, 11 am to 11 pm on Saturday and 12 noon to 3 pm and 7 pm to 10.30 pm on Sunday. Food is served daily from 12 noon to 2 pm and 7 pm to 9.30 pm (9 pm on Sunday). Telephone: 01892 783224.

- **HOW TO GET THERE:** From the A267 Eastbourne-to-Tunbridge Wells road, access to Wadhurst is via the B2100 at Mark Cross or the B2099 south of Frant. From the other direction (east) Wadhurst can be reached from the A21 Tunbridge Wells-to-Hastings road, using the B2100 from Lamberhurst or the B2087 at Flimwell, joining the B2099 at Ticehurst.
- **PARKING:** Park in the larger of two free car parks in the centre of the village, signposted from the main street beside the Greyhound pub.
- **LENGTH OF THE WALK:** 6½ miles. Map: OS Explorer 136 The Weald (GR 641309).

THE WALK

1. To start the walk, make your way to the church, go through the main gateway and keep to the right edge of the churchyard. After less than 100 yards, fork right by a 'No cycling' notice and follow an enclosed path through to a lane. Turn right along the lane and, where it goes squarely right, turn left along the roughly metalled drive to Little Pell Farm, passing a large hop field on your right. Pass to the left of two barns and continue with a hedge and fence, left. A well defined rough track begins to drop down between sandy banks, rich with wild foxgloves in the early summer. The track

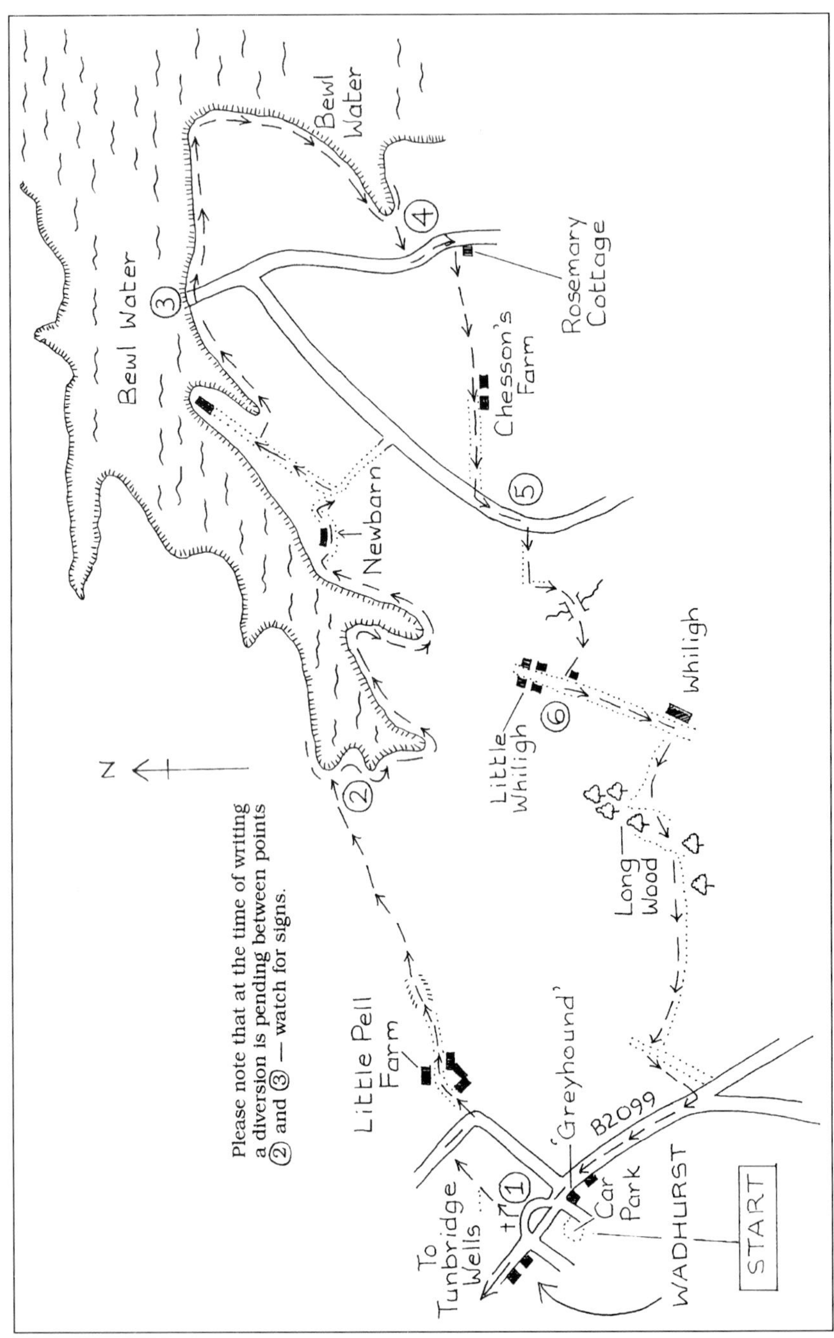
Bewl Water
Bewl Water
Rosemary Cottage
Chesson's Farm
Newbarn
Whiligh
Little Whiligh
Long Wood
Little Pell Farm
'Greyhound'
B2099
Car Park
To Tunbridge Wells
WADHURST
START
N
1
2
3
4
5
6
Please note that at the time of writing a diversion is pending between points ② and ③ — watch for signs.

The return route between points 5 and 6

narrows to a path and takes you down to a T-junction with a wider track.

Please note that at the time of writing a diversion is pending between the next two points (2 and 3) – watch for signs.

2. Turn right, now on the reservoir perimeter path with the water soon in sight through trees and scrub on your left. After the best part of a mile the reservoir path diverts away from the water's edge, skirting to the right of the house and converted oast at Newbarn. Follow the drive from the house uphill until you can turn left along the concrete drive to Bryant's Farm. Although not signed as a right of way, it is a public footpath. On reaching a gateway, turn right over a stile, this time signposted as a footpath to Hook Hill.

3. Go straight across the end of an old road disappearing under the waters of the reservoir and shortly fork right up steps on a path which provides a drier alternative to a lower route which tends to flood when the water level is high. The waterside path continues with intermittent views across the reservoir to the dam and boat launching areas. After rounding a point a completely new view of another finger of the reservoir opens up.

4. Where the path doubles back to the left at the end of a narrow inlet of the reservoir, you should go ahead through a gate and along a short path which takes you out to a lane. Turn left and, after about 250 yards, turn right along the concrete access to Rosemary Cottage. Go ahead through a gate, leaving the cottage on your left, and continue forward along the right edge of two fields with a high hedge on your right. At Chesson's Farm pass between the buildings, then go ahead along the farm access drive to join a lane and turn left.

5. After about 200 yards, go right through a gate and follow a sunken grassy headland down into a valley. At the field corner, go through a gateway and turn left, still on a shallow sunken track. At the bottom of the hill go ahead through a gate, over a stream and on along a defined grassy strip between low banks. It becomes less clear as it climbs, veering slightly right to join a drive through a gate to the right of a single-storey brick cottage.

6. Turn left along this concrete drive. After almost 1/4 mile, turn right down steps, through a kissing gate and down into another valley with the spire of Wadhurst church in view ahead. Follow a fence on your right at first. Towards the bottom of the hill veer half left to find a stile in a crossing fence in the valley bottom. A clear path continues through Long Wood, a fine area of open oak woodland. Go through a gate, cross a footbridge and, where you have a choice of mown paths, keep left and climb with trees and scrub on your left. A trodden headland path with a fence, left, climbs steadily. Cross a drive and the stile opposite and veer half left across a field to join the B2099. Turn right for 1/2 mile, back into Wadhurst.

PLACES OF INTEREST NEARBY

The *Bewl Water Visitor Centre*, on the northern shore of the reservoir, is accessible from the B2100 road between Wadhurst and Lamberhurst. It incorporates information about the reservoir, an adventure playground and a refreshment kiosk, open in summer. From April to October the SS *Frances Mary* provides cruises with an opportunity to disembark and walk back to the Centre. If you are feeling really energetic you can hire a bicycle and complete the entire 13 mile perimeter cycle route. Telephone: 01892 890661.

WALK 16

BEACHY HEAD AND BELLE TOUT

Although more of a 'high above the water' than a waterside walk, this is a superb circuit, contrasting an exhilarating cliff top stroll with an inland return route across rolling chalk downland and through a sheltered combe. A short, sharp climb brings us back up onto the 530 ft summit of Beachy Head.

Belle Tout from Beachy Head

The dramatic line of chalk cliffs between Eastbourne and Seaford, where the ridge of the South Downs is abruptly cut off by a precipitous plunge to the sea, provide exceptional walking. Almost the whole of this 12 mile 'Heritage Coast' is now in public or quasi-public ownership and protected from inappropriate development. On this walk we are quickly away from the busy tourist area on the top of Beachy Head to follow a cliff top path to the old lighthouse of Belle Tout. Built in 1831, it was superseded by the new light at the foot of Beachy Head. As the chalk cliffs recede year by year, Belle Tout is now in danger of falling into the sea and ambitious plans are afoot to jack it up and move it bodily away from the edge. After a hefty cliff fall during the winter of 1998/99 left it teetering on the brink, it is touch and go whether it will collapse before it can be moved. The second half of the walk takes us inland through part of the 4,000 acre area of the Downs owned by Eastbourne Borough. The whole of this downland estate is now managed in a sensitive way with less intensive cultivation and more grazing, giving us, in places, just a glimpse of how the Downs looked back in the 1920s. There are still too many fences but even these are being replaced by temporary electric barriers punctuated with portable gates for access.

Towards the end of the walk, you can divert to the Beachy Head pub if you can face the crowds. Rebuilt a few years ago after being destroyed by fire, it is now a big 'Brewer's Fayre' eating house, seating 300, with a separate coffee shop next door. The food is what you would expect from a large pub chain, and the beer is good enough – three real ales on hand pump including Wadworth 6X, Boddingtons Bitter plus changing guest beers. The opening hours are extensive, summer and winter: Monday to Saturday from 11 am to 11 pm and on Sunday from 12 noon to 10.30 pm. Food is available from 11.30 am to 10 pm on weekdays and from 12 noon to 10 pm on Sundays. The coffee shop is open daily from 10 am to 5 pm in summer. Telephone: 01323 728060.

- **HOW TO GET THERE:** Beachy Head is signposted along the B2103 from the A259 coast road about a mile out of Eastbourne. Fork right along an unclassified road and follow it past the Beachy Head pub and on towards Birling Gap.
- **PARKING:** Park in either of two roadside parking areas on the Beachy Head-to-Birling Gap road about 1/4 mile west of the Beachy Head pub and Countryside Centre. There is a regular summer bus service to Beachy Head from Eastbourne town centre.
- **LENGTH OF THE WALK:** 6 1/4 miles. Map: OS Explorer 123 (previously 16) South Downs Way – Newhaven to Eastbourne (GR 586957 or GR 584954).

THE WALK

1. From whichever car park you use, walk out to the edge of the cliff and turn right. The whole strip between cliff edge and road is

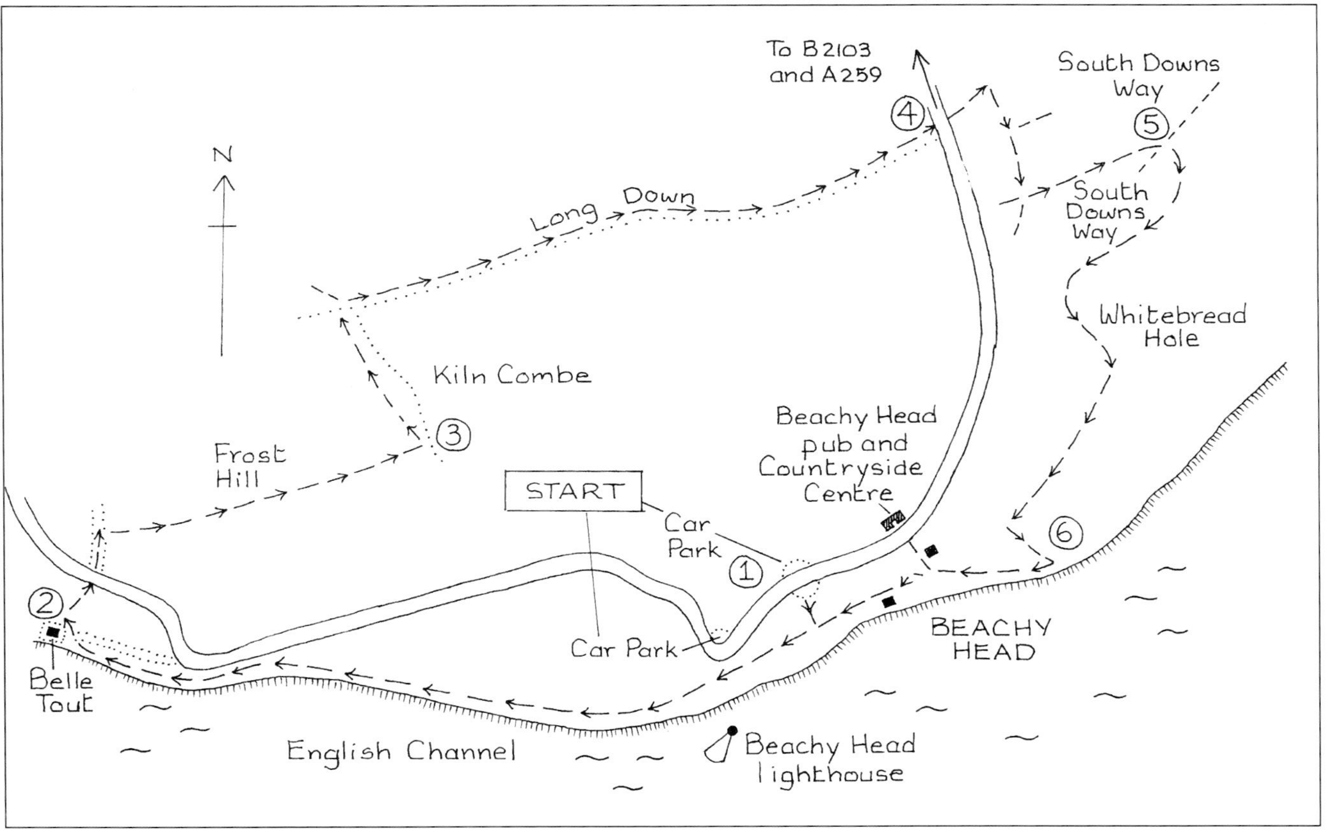
To B2103
and A259
South Downs
Way
4
5
N
Long Down
South
Downs
Way
Whitebread
Hole
Kiln Combe
Beachy Head
pub and
Countryside
Centre
3
Frost
Hill
START
Car
Park
6
1
2
BEACHY
HEAD
Car Park
Belle
Tout
English Channel
Beachy Head
lighthouse

The old lighthouse at Belle Tout

open for public access, allowing you to pick your route and also adding a dimension of openness and freedom. The cliff is crumbling away so keep well away from the edge. There are one or two places from which you can get a safe glimpse of the new Beachy Head lighthouse at the foot of the cliffs and there are glorious views ahead to Belle Tout, the Seven Sisters and, in the far distance, Seaford Head rising up on the other side of Cuckmere Haven. Follow the cliff edge westwards through two dips and up to the old Belle Tout lighthouse, keeping to the landward side of the building and surrounding enclosure.

2. When you are level with the far corner of the walled lighthouse enclosure, turn squarely right and drop steeply downhill between gorse and scrub to the road and follow the concrete drive to Cornish Farm, opposite. After 100 yards turn right along a headland path, signposted to Eastbourne, climbing steadily on to Frost Hill with a fence, left.

3. After almost $^{3}/_{4}$ mile, in the field corner, turn left through a bridle gate, go ahead over a summit to a second bridle gate and then drop steeply down into Kiln Combe and up the other side. At the top of the slope, go through a gate and turn right to follow a clear bridleway along the low ridge of Long Down for over a mile.

4. Cross the Beachy Head road and follow the signed bridleway opposite with Eastbourne spread out ahead of you and, beyond, along the coast on a clear day, the power station at Dungeness. After 150 yards, at a waypost, turn right along a gently rising path with a scrub-covered slope dropping away to your left. Ignore paths to the left until, after 300 yards, you come to a waypost with a blue arrow pointing ahead and yellow arrows to right and left. Go left here and drop gently down on a wide grassy strip between scattered scrub with the sea directly ahead.

5. On reaching a South Downs Way post, you have a choice. The most direct and easier route is to the right along the South Downs Way. For a more interesting alternative, go straight ahead on a path which curves right and drops down before contouring round the lower slopes of a scrub-covered combe (Whitebread Hole). A good path continues along the lower hillside before turning squarely left towards the sea.

6. At the cliff edge, turn right and climb steeply up onto Beachy Head. At the top there is an area protected by railings from which you get an excellent view of the crumbling chalk cliffs and the new Beachy Head lighthouse. To visit the pub, go straight ahead here past the highest point, but to complete the walk bear left round another small combe and on past the remains of a tower, used by Lloyd's as a signal station at the end of the 19th century. In more recent times, at least until the late 1950s, there was a large Air Ministry signal station on the site. Continue along the cliff path until you can turn away from the sea directly back to your car park.

Places of Interest Nearby

The *Beachy Head Countryside Centre*, incorporated in the new pub building, provides an excellent introduction to the history, geology and wild life of the area, using up to the minute audio-visual techniques, including an animated 'talking shepherd' and a 3-D slide show as well as models and video and computer presentations. It is open daily, though times vary with the season. Telephone: 01323 737273.

WALK 17

BODIAM CASTLE AND THE EASTERN ROTHER

The medieval castle at Bodiam provides the focus of this walk beside the Eastern Rother and over higher ground to the south of the valley. It is a relatively short and easy circuit, allowing time and energy to visit the castle and climb to the top of the battlements.

Bodiam Castle

The Eastern Rother rises deep in the High Weald and flows eastwards before opening out into a wide valley beyond Robertsbridge, where the moated castle at Bodiam is strategically placed to control the river and overlook a gap in the low hills. The Rother was navigable as far as Bodiam Bridge when, in 1377, Sir Edward Dalyngrigge was granted a licence to fortify his manor house against invaders. Subsequently the castle was besieged during the Wars of the Roses and dismantled during the Civil War. For the present restoration as a romantic ruin, we can thank Lord Curzon who bought the property in 1917 and bequeathed it, on his death, to the National Trust. From across the moat the castle appears almost intact and offers a fine prospect, particularly the 60 foot towers of the imposing entrance gatehouse. A walk round the moat offers one of the finest waterside strolls in Sussex which you can enjoy before or after the main walk. Go out of season to avoid the crowds who lay siege to the castle in the summer months.

The landlord of the Castle Inn at Bodiam claims that there has been a pub on the site as long as there has been a castle, though the present building is a mere 200 years old. It offers excellent beer on hand pump and an extensive food menu including several interesting vegetarian dishes. All the usual bar snacks are available, plus some exotic variations such as speciality sausages with wild boar, venison and ostrich fillings. Alternatively you can sample local duck eggs, fried or scrambled with ham or smoked salmon. The opening hours are extensive, commencing with breakfast from 10 am, right through till 10 pm, with food served throughout the day. Telephone: 01580 830330.

- **HOW TO GET THERE:** From Hawkhurst on the Kent border to the north via the B2244 and an unclassified road; or from Hastings to the south using the A21, B2244 and B2165 to Staplecross, then an unclassified signposted road.
- **PARKING:** In the large Bodiam Castle car park (fee payable, free to National Trust members).
- **LENGTH OF THE WALK:** 4 miles. Map: OS Explorer 136 The Weald (GR 783254).

The Walk

1. From the entrance to the car park, turn left across the River Rother and after a few more yards, go left again, doubling back to follow the raised river bank. After about 300 yards, just short of a gate, turn right to walk squarely away from the river with a drainage ditch to your left. In the field corner, follow the field edge round to the right until you can go left through a gate, across the track bed of the old Kent and East Sussex Railway, left over a stile and, after a few yards, right, passing to the right of a Dutch barn to cross a footbridge and go ahead along a right field edge. In the field corner go over another footbridge and forward with a fence on your left, ignoring a stile in this fence and climbing gently out of the valley. At

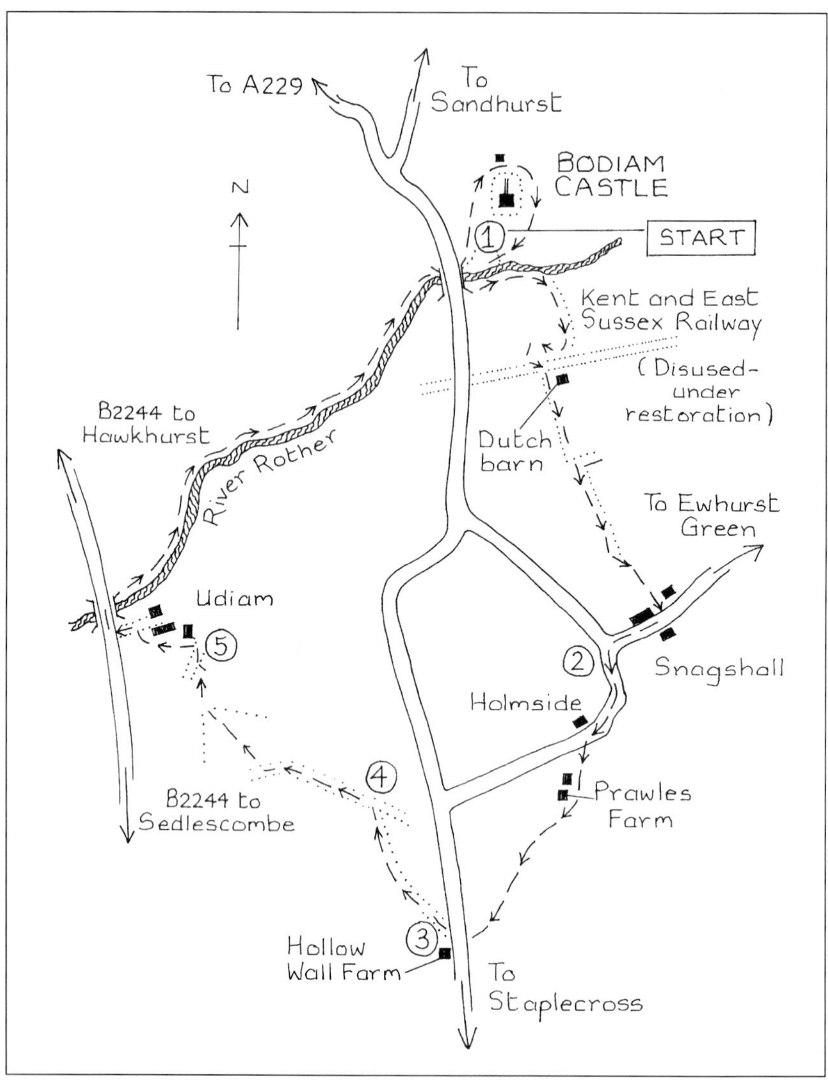

the top field corner go left through a gate, right to a stile and on along an enclosed path out to a lane where you should turn right.

2. At a road junction, bear left, signposted to Staplecross, and after another 350 yards, opposite a house called Holmside on the right, you should go left over a stile and bear half right, soon veering left by a waypost, across pasture to a stile beside a gate. Once over this stile, turn right along the field edge, following it round to the left until you can go right through a gate and forward along a headland to another gate. Cross the next field, veering very slightly left rather than along the obvious path ahead. Go over a stile beside a gate and keep to the right of the field beyond. In the field corner go over a stile, veering half right across a field to join a lane.

3. Turn right and, after a few yards, fork left along a rough fenced track. Beyond a gate, veer half right, climbing and contouring along the hillside with a hedge on your right and a magnificent view to the north-west across the Rother valley. After about 1/4 mile, a stile on the right provides access into an enclosed hedged path, marked as Udiam Lane on OS maps.

4. Turn left and follow this ancient track between low banks. After about 350 yards, fork right over a stile and head diagonally out across a newly planted orchard where there is no sign of a path though the trees are conveniently aligned to allow you to pass between them. In the far corner, go over another stile, through a bridle gate and drop down along a left field edge until you can sidestep to the left to join and continue downhill on a wide track.

5. Just short of the first buildings at Udiam, turn left along a track. After a few yards, go over a stile on the left and resume your direction downhill with a fence on your right, passing a small stable with attached dovecotes. At the bottom two stiles provide access to the drive from Udiam on which you should turn left out to the B2244. Turn right, cross the Rother and go right again to follow the river bank for a mile or so back to the start.

Places of Interest Nearby

Bodiam Castle (National Trust) is open daily from approximately February to the end of October between 10 am and 6 pm, and from November to January on Tuesday to Sunday between 10 am and 4 pm or dusk if earlier. Telephone: 01580 830436. *Bedgebury Pinetum*, a few miles to the north via Hawkhurst, incorporates the national conifer collection and is managed by the Forestry Commission in conjunction with Kew Gardens. The gardens, which also provide a display of rhododendrons and azaleas in the spring, are open daily from 10 am to 7 pm or dusk if earlier.

WALK 18

HASTINGS COUNTRY PARK

A short but relatively strenuous walk, much of it along sea cliffs within the Hastings Country Park. The paths are very well maintained and signs and steps are provided to help with the steeper climbs. An excellent family walk within easy reach of the resort town of Hastings.

Above Ecclesbourne Glen

The coastline to the east of Hastings, with its unique fossil-rich geology, combining high cliffs, secluded wooded glens and open heathland, provides splendid, if rather strenuous, walking. The entire 640 acre area of the Hastings Country Park is now protected as a designated Site of Special Scientific Interest. The cliffs, comprising a mixture of sand and clay, are eroding at a rate of over a metre each year, and are subject to regular landslip, so care must be taken to keep to the marked cliff path which, over the years, has had to be shifted gradually inland as the cliff has subsided. One well known Victorian viewpoint, at Lover's Seat, has disappeared into the sea.

The whole area is rich in wild life, including seabirds such as fulmars which nest on the cliffs and heathland birds like stonechats, yellowhammers and whitethroats. The deep, humid glens offer a microclimate which allows rare ferns and lichens to thrive.

From a car park on the edge of Hastings, the walk drops quickly down into Ecclesbourne Glen and then follows a switchback route eastwards over the cliffs, with two more steep 'down and ups' at Fairlight and Warren Glens. From Fairlight Glen you can get down onto the beach, but access to the sea elsewhere is prevented by cliff erosion. For the return route the walk crosses high ground with fine seaward views.

This is the only walk in the book without a pub either on or very near the route. The pub marked on OS maps in Barley Lane near the start of the walk no longer exists. Your best bet is to drive down into Hastings Old Town, well worth a visit in its own right (see Places of Interest Nearby). There you will find several pubs as well as cafés and fish restaurants. If you are feeling very energetic, you might like to approach the Old Town on foot. From point 2 on the walk, head west across the open cliff top of East Hill for just over 1/2 mile. If your timing is right, there is a cliff railway to take you down to sea level and back up again after your refreshment break.

- **HOW TO GET THERE:** From the A259 Hastings-to-Rye road at the eastern end of Hastings, 1/4 mile up the hill from the Old Town, turn right along Barley Lane or Gurth Road leading into Barley Lane.
- **PARKING:** In the Hastings Country Park Barley Lane car park to the right of the lane after a little over 1/2 mile.
- **LENGTH OF THE WALK:** 3 3/4 miles. Map: OS Explorer 124 Hastings and Bexhill (GR 838105).

THE WALK

1. From the back of the car park, about 10 yards to the left of the right hand corner, go through a gap in a post and rail fence and follow a clear path which veers right. Ignore a downhill fork to the left and continue on a fine grassy path which contours along the hillside at first with a fine view through the cleft of Ecclesbourne Glen to the sea. Follow the main path along the increasingly wooded side of the glen, gradually losing height.

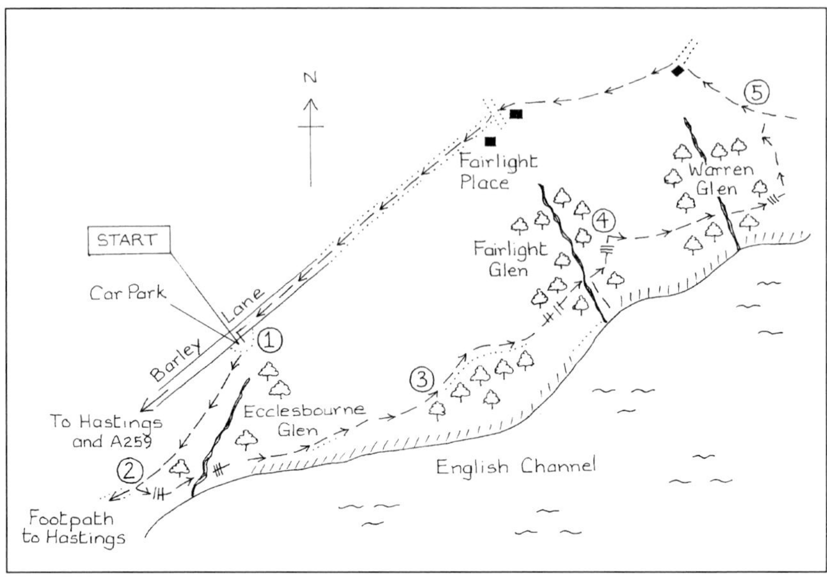

2. After about 700 yards, turn left down an elaborate flight of steps. At a path junction fork right down more steps, almost to the mouth of Ecclesbourne Glen where a notice warns that there is no access to the beach due to erosion of the crumbling cliffs. Climb another set of steps, steeply out of the glen. It is hard work but height is quickly gained. Halfway up there is a well placed seat from which to look back along the cliffs towards Hastings. At the top, on emerging from the scrub, go ahead on a clear grassy path along the top of the cliffs but set well back from the scrub-covered cliff edge.

3. Beyond a large wooden bollard, one of several encountered on this walk, go ahead on a wide path which climbs across higher ground. Where the path divides, fork right, soon dropping down more steps into Fairlight Glen. At the bottom, fork right, signposted to Lover's Seat and Firehills. Cross a stream where a path on the right provides safe access to the beach, and climb steeply out of the glen, with further rewarding views from another seat.

4. At the next bollard, turn sharply back to the right up more steps to reach the cliff summit. After a short open grassy path, steps take you down into Warren Glen and straight up the other side. About halfway up, at the top of a short flight of steps with a handrail, you

The cliffs near Fairlight Glen

will come to a T-junction. Turn left for 5 yards only past a seat before going right and resuming your climb steadily up the side of the glen, now walking away from the sea.

5. At the top, turn left along a broad crossing path coming from the coastguard station, away to your right. The path contours along the head of Warren Glen. Go obliquely across the end of a cottage access track to find a stile and waypost indicating a path to Barley Lane. Follow this well waymarked and stiled field path which takes a straight course across high ground with fine seaward views, becoming a hedged path and then a roughly metalled access drive. At a junction with another drive, go ahead, still on a drive, which leads into Barley Lane and back to the start.

Places of Interest Nearby

Hastings Old Town is notable for a number of carefully preserved and visually striking tall black timber huts used for drying and storing nets. All that remains of an intended harbour, begun in 1896 but never completed, is a stone breakwater. The fishing boats are now pulled up onto the shingle beach. Nearby is a *Fishermen's Museum*.

WALK 19

THE ROYAL MILITARY CANAL AND THE BREDE VALLEY

From the charming little hilltop town of Winchelsea this walk drops quickly down onto an area of reclaimed marshland to follow a mile of the disused Royal Military Canal. A gentle climb to higher ground leads to Icklesham with its well placed pub. The return route descends again to join the River Brede as it flows along the floor of a beautiful open valley. A final short sharp climb brings us back to the start.

The River Brede

The Royal Military Canal was built between 1804 and 1806 in the face of Napoleon's invasion threat and subsequently carried freight in horse-drawn barges between Hythe and Rye, finally falling into disuse after 1877. During World War II it was brought back into use as a coastal defence. Originally a road ran along the landward side, protected from enemy fire by a parapet of excavated soil. In recent years a new footpath route has been developed along the whole length of the canal from Hythe in Kent to the sea at Cliff End south of Winchelsea.

The Brede is a modest river but has carved out a broad valley between low Wealden ridges as it flows from its source near Sedlescombe to the north of Hastings eastwards to join the Eastern Rother at Rye. This walk allows us to enjoy sections of both canal and river, crossing higher ground between the two waterways to visit the village of Icklesham which provides a welcome refreshment stop about halfway round the circuit.

The Queen's Head occupies a superb site on the edge of Icklesham overlooking the Brede valley. The building dates from 1632 and has served as a pub for over 150 years. The beamed interior on two levels has open fireplaces and is decorated with dried hops and old farm implements. The pub offers CAMRA-recommended beers from the local Pett and Rother Valley breweries as well as from Greene King and other sources. There is a regular menu of solid pub fare, all home made, plus blackboard specials, sandwiches and five different varieties of ploughman's. The opening hours on Monday to Saturday are from 11 am to 11 pm and on Sunday from 12 noon to 10.30 pm. Food is served on Monday to Thursday from 12 noon to 2.45 pm and from 6.30 pm to 9.45 pm and on Friday to Sunday from 11.45 am to 9.45 pm. Telephone: 01424 814552.

- **HOW TO GET THERE:** The village of Winchelsea is on the A259 Hastings-to-Rye road, about 2 miles from Rye.
- **PARKING:** There is fairly generous roadside parking in Winchelsea but no official car park.
- **LENGTH OF THE WALK:** 6 miles. Map: OS Explorer 125 Romney Marsh or 124 Hastings and Bexhill (GR 904174).

The Walk

1. Start the walk from the New Inn at the north-west corner of Winchelsea churchyard and head east, leaving the Court Hall and Museum on your left and the church on your right. Take the second turning on the left and, where the road veers to the left, go ahead on a narrow path which soon drops down a flight of stone steps to join the A259. Cross the road with great care as the path comes out on a blind bend, and turn right along the opposite pavement.

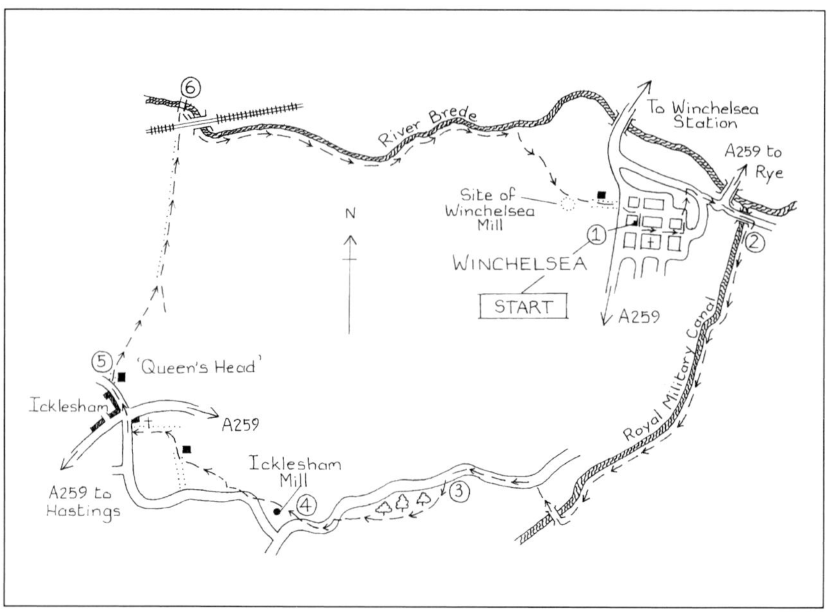

Follow the road past the Bridge Inn and after a few yards go right, signed to Winchelsea Beach.

2. After 60 yards turn right over a stile where a waypost indicates that you are joining the Royal Military Canal Path to Cliff End. Follow the canal bank for about a mile until you can turn right over a broad concrete bridge and walk along a left field edge up to join a lane and turn left.

3. After about 450 yards go left through a gate and along a wide unfenced track. From here to Icklesham you will be following part of another long-distance path, the 1066 Country Walk, indicated by a red logo. From this raised path there are excellent views across Pett Level to the sea and eastwards along the coast to Dungeness Power Station. Looking ahead you can pick out the tower of Fairlight church high above the cliffs to the east of Hastings (Walk 18). Continue on a clear path through to join a lane and bear left along it.

4. After a little over 100 yards fork right through a gate and follow a

The Royal Military Canal

grassy path skirting to the right of Icklesham Mill, descending again to rejoin the lane once more. Bear right along the lane and, after a few yards, go right through a gate and left along the edge of an orchard. Follow waymarks right and left through the orchard to join a drive and turn right past the elaborately converted Manor Farm Oast, shortly forking left on a grassy path. Follow this path, passing an access on the right to Icklesham church, worth a detour if time permits. At a lane turn right and shortly cross the A259 and follow the cul-de-sac opposite.

5. Skirt to the left of the Queen's Head pub and walk through the pub car park to find a stile to the right of a static caravan. Follow the direction of a sign to a gate and on down a grassy slope into the Brede valley with a good view of Rye at the end of the valley to the right. At the bottom of the slope go over a cattle grid and forward with a drainage ditch on your left. Cross the railway and go ahead for a few yards to reach a bridge over the River Brede.

6. Don't cross the bridge. Instead, turn right and follow the river, crossing back over the railway. After about a mile beside the river you will come to a stile with a yellow arrow on it indicating that the

The remains of Winchelsea Mill

path diverges from the river bank. Bear half right to a gate and a three-arm signpost, then veer half right again to a stile in the top right field corner. From here a grassy hollow way takes you up past a trig point on a mound once occupied by Winchelsea Mill. In ruins for many years, it was finally swept away during the Great Gale of 1987. The site is now a fine viewpoint overlooking the Brede valley. Continue to join a drive which takes you out to the A259. Follow the road opposite back into Winchelsea.

Places of Interest Nearby

Before or after the walk, allow time to explore the ancient Cinque Port of *Winchelsea*. The town, once with a harbour but now set well back from the coast, was laid out in a grid pattern when it was rebuilt in the 12th century. The old Court Hall now houses a small museum and the church, built in 14th-century decorated style, is a striking fragment of a much larger building, never completed. Three of the gates built in the town wall still survive.

WALK 20

RYE HARBOUR NATURE RESERVE

For the whole of this circuit you will be walking across completely level ground, once submerged by the sea, mostly with grass-covered shingle underfoot. You will have an opportunity to observe plants unique to this spartan habitat and to view a remarkable selection of bird species from well placed bird hides. The waterside interest is provided by a labyrinth of waterfilled gravel pits and a final stroll along the foreshore.

Rye Harbour

Established as a nature reserve in 1970 and designated as a Site of Special Scientific Interest, Rye Harbour Nature Reserve is made up of a number of habitats including tidal saltmarsh, grazed marshland and, most importantly, a series of shingle ridges, supporting plant species, some rare or endangered, which have adapted to survive in this hostile environment. If, like me, you are not a good natural historian, take a flower identification book and look out for sea kale, red valerian, yellow horned poppy, sea pea and viper's bugloss. The whole area is dotted with disused and flooded gravel pits which provide a home for over 270 species of bird of which 70 breed in the area so you will need a bird book and a good pair of binoculars too.

Camber Castle, which once stood on a shingle spit overlooking the sea, was built in 1540 by Henry VIII as one of five blockhouses designed to fend off a papally inspired invasion by Francis I of France. In 1642, as the sea receded, it was abandoned and partially dismantled. In recent years English Heritage have made it safe for public access and it is now open occasionally during the summer months.

The William the Conqueror at Rye Harbour is a fairly basic modern pub which looks as if it has been adapted from a private residence. There are three Shepherd Neame beers on hand pump, Bishops Finger, Spitfire and Master Brew, and the food on offer includes some unusual dishes such as chicken, asparagus and wine pie. The snack menu includes baguettes and sandwiches with locally caught crab among the fillings. Opening hours on Monday to Saturday are from 12 noon to 11 pm and on Sunday from 12 noon to 10.30 pm. Food is available from 12 noon to 2.30 pm and 7 pm to 9.30 pm daily. Telephone: 01797 223315.

- **HOW TO GET THERE:** Rye Harbour is signposted along an unclassified road from the A259 Rye-to-Hastings road immediately to the south of Rye.
- **PARKING:** There is a large free car park at Rye Harbour.
- **LENGTH OF THE WALK:** 5¾ miles. Map: OS Explorer 125 Romney Marsh (GR 942189).

THE WALK

1. From the car park, turn left, walking back along the main road towards Rye but allowing time for a short detour out to the harbour area beside the River Rother and back. Follow the Rye road past the rather unusual looking church, set back from the road on the left. In the churchyard is a poignant memorial to the 17 crew members of the lifeboat *Mary Stanford*, lost during a rescue operation in November 1928.

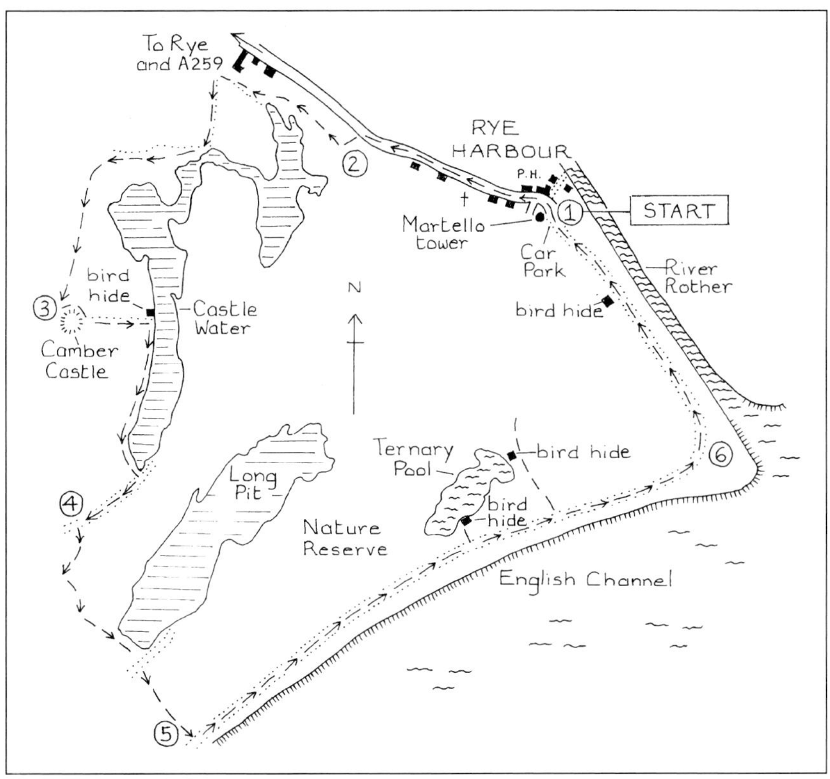

2. About 500 yards past the church, look out for a path on the left, indicated by a waypost. Follow this clear and well signed route as it skirts round the back of an industrial area, eventually picking up and following a fence to the left. Keep beside this fence as it turns sharply left, ignoring a path to the right. Beyond a stile, go forward, now walking parallel to a fence on your right, with a flooded gravel pit away to your left. Beyond a stile beside a gate, continue with a fence on your left. Once over another stile, follow a faint unfenced track towards Camber Castle.

3. Just short of the castle, follow a waymark to the left, walking beneath the castle walls to a stile. Beyond the stile, turn left beside a fence on your left. In the field corner, where two stiles provide access to a bird hide overlooking Castle Water, you should turn right, soon walking beside the water on your left. After rounding the end of Castle Water you will come to a T-junction with a broad track where you should turn right.

4. After about 350 yards, with the buildings of Castle Farm in view about 250 yards ahead, turn left over a stile and follow a left field edge. At a crossing track where there is a waypost, turn left and, after a few yards, ignore a left fork. Very shortly, go ahead on a grassy path, ignoring the main track which forks left. Ignore another track to the left and at a T-junction go left to cross a stile beside a gate and continue with a fence, left, to a second gate/stile combination. Now go forward with a large expanse of water to your left (Long Pit). Cross a shingle track and head towards the sea on the top of a raised bank.

5. On reaching a metalled road, turn left. You now have a choice. You can follow the road, walk along the top of the high shingle bank between the road and the sea, or, if the tide is right, drop down the other side and follow the foreshore. For variety, you can combine a bit of all three. You will pass the old lifeboat station and, a little further on, accessible by footpath landwards from the road, two public bird hides overlooking the Ternary Pool. From here you can observe a variety of nesting birds during the spring and summer, including the rare little tern as well as the common tern, black headed gull and little grebe.

6. Whichever route you use, you will come to the mouth of the River Rother where you must turn inland and follow the road back to Rye Harbour, passing another bird hide on your left. Beside the car park at the end of the walk stands one of the few remaining martello towers, built in 1807 as part of the defences against the threat of invasion by Napoleon. With walls more than 12 feet thick on the seaward side, the towers were designed to house and protect a garrison of 25.

PLACES OF INTEREST NEARBY

The ancient towns of *Rye* and *Winchelsea*, once important sea ports from which the sea has receded, are within easy reach. Both are strikingly situated on hilltops overlooking drained marshland. Both have impressive churches, reflecting their one time status as Cinque Ports.